Explorers, Missionaries, and Trappers

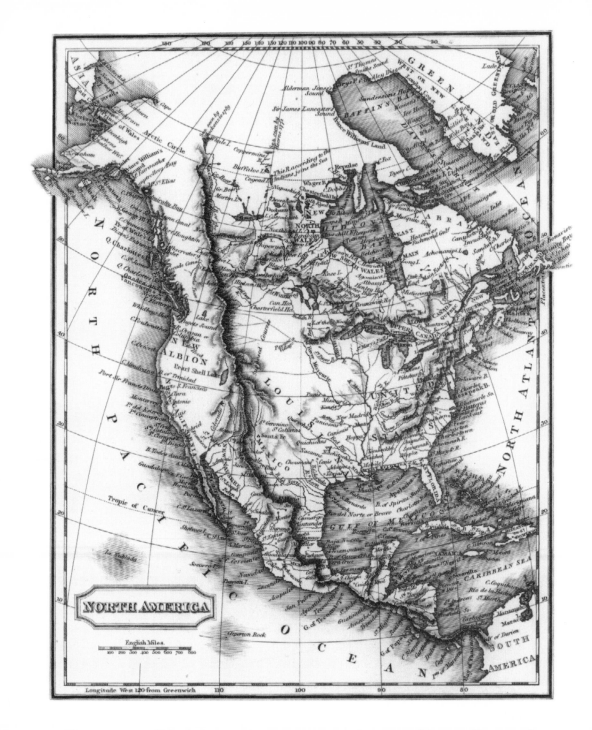

This 1816 map of North America shows a continent in the process of change. "Louisiana" had been purchased from France by the United States 13 years before, but England still had claim on the Northwest "New Albion" and Spain held California and much of the Southwest.

Explorers, Missionaries, and Trappers

Trailblazers of the West

Kieran Doherty

The Oliver Press, Inc.
Minneapolis

The publisher wishes to thank Don Garate, chief of interpretation/historian at Tumacacori National Historical Park, for his careful review of the Eusebio Kino chapter.

The Oliver Press, Inc.
Charlotte Square
5707 West 36th Street
Minneapolis, MN 55416-2510

Library of Congress Cataloging-in-Publication Data
Doherty, Kieran.
Explorers, missionaries, and trappers : trailblazers of the West / Kieran Doherty.
p.   cm.—(Shaping America ; 3)
Includes bibliographical references and index.
    Summary: Presents the founding of the American West through the lives of explorers and settlers such as Eusebio Kino in Arizona, Junípero Serra in Spanish California, and Brigham Young in Utah.
ISBN 1-881508-52-8 (lib. bdg.)
1. Pioneers—West (U.S.)—Biography—Juvenile literature. 2. West (U.S.)—Biography—Juvenile literature. 3. Frontier and pioneer life—West (U.S.)—Juvenile literature. 4. Explorers—West (U.S.)—Biography—Juvenile literature. 5. Missionaries—West (U.S.)—Biography—Juvenile literature. 6. Trappers—West (U.S.)—Biography—Juvenile literature. [1. Pioneers. 2. Explorers. 3. Missionaries. 4. West (U.S.)—Biography. 5. Frontier and pioneer life—West (U.S.)] I. Title. II. Series.
F591.D64   2000
978'.009'9—dc21
[B]   98-54636
                                        CIP
                                        AC
ISBN 1-881508-52-8
Printed in the United States of America
06 05 04 03 02 01 00   8 7 6 5 4 3 2 1

Contents

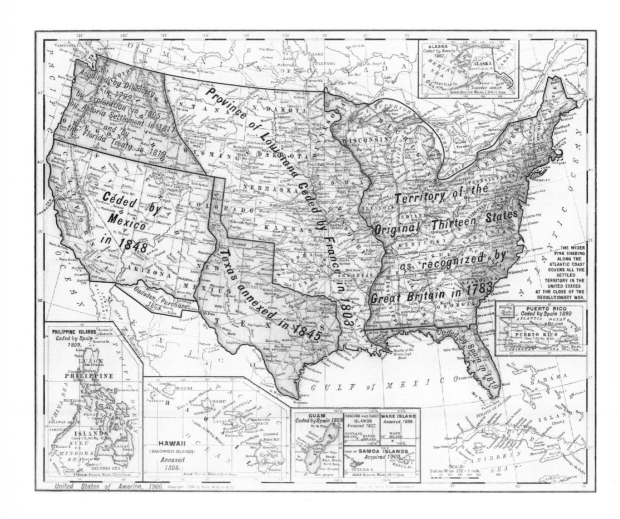

Introduction

❦

For centuries before the first European set
foot in the vast region we know today as
the western United States, the land was home to
thousands of American Indians. Two groups, the
Hohokams and the Anasazis, were particularly
important. Based in Arizona, the Hohokams were
successful farmers who built cities and developed
systems of aqueducts to irrigate dry lands hundreds
of years before the first Europeans arrived in the
New World. The agricultural Anasazis were mostly
cliff dwellers who lived along the Rio Grande and
Colorado River in the Southwest.

As time passed, the Hohokams and Anasazis
evolved into tribes whose names are more familiar,
including the Pimas and Pueblos of Arizona and
New Mexico. Some of the other important Indians
of the West were the Flatheads and Nez Perces of
the Northwest, the Utes and Shoshones of Utah and
Idaho, and the Navajo of Arizona.

For nearly a thousand generations, Indians of
the West hunted, fished, and traded, unaware of the
existence of a world across the seas. Although they

*This map of the United States
provides a blueprint of the
changing shape of the nation.
Added lands would double the
original territory a quarter
century after the nation's
founding and triple the
holdings in less than 70 years.*

This village from the eleventh century is one of several hundred in Canyon de Chelly in northeast Arizona. Generations of Anasazis added on extra rooms and upper stories to their buildings.

Christopher Columbus was not the first explorer to reach the New World. Phoenicians from the Middle East may have come 2,000 years ago, and Vikings from northern Europe sailed to American shores around A.D. 1000.

had no way of knowing it at the time, that began to change in 1492 when Christopher Columbus sailed to the New World. After stumbling onto the Americas as he searched for a sea route to the Far East, Columbus established an outpost at Santo Domingo in the present-day Dominican Republic. From that base, Spanish explorers quickly fanned out through the Caribbean and then over large parts of the Americas.

Juan Ponce de León began the exploration and conquest of North America when he landed in Florida in 1513. Within just a few decades, Spanish explorers and colonists had crossed the Isthmus of Panama to the Pacific Ocean, sailed around the world for the first time, conquered the Aztecs in Mexico and the Incas in Peru, explored parts of Texas, New Mexico, and Arizona, and marched north from Mexico as far as present-day Kansas.

This book begins with the stories of two Spaniards and another priest in Spanish service. While Juan de Oñate sought wealth for Spain in New Mexico, the other two men wanted to spread their religion to the Indians of the West. Austrian-born Eusebio Kino, a Jesuit priest, became the first

The first permanent European settlement in North America was St. Augustine, Florida, founded in 1565 by Spaniard Pedro Menéndez de Avilés.

Aztec emperor Moctezuma (or Montezuma) surrendered to Hernán Cortés and his men in 1519. Moctezuma's empire in Mexico was larger than Spain and had more than twice the population.

missionary in Arizona, and Father Junípero Serra, a Franciscan, founded nine missions in California.

The Pacific Coast of North America was difficult to reach from Europe because it required a long and dangerous sea voyage around the southernmost tip of South America. For that reason, western settlements in the seventeenth and eighteenth centuries were, for the most part, limited to those founded in the Southwest by the Spanish, who traveled north and west overland from Mexico.

In the nineteenth century, however, the whole course of settlement in the West changed as the young American republic stretched its muscles and began expanding from the Mississippi River over the Rocky Mountains and into the western territories. This expansion started slowly as explorers, including Meriwether Lewis and William Clark, mapped what was then a mysterious land. The maps made it possible for fur traders, missionaries, and settlers to make their way across the continent. Within just a few years, Americans from the East began founding new towns in the West. Clashes soon followed with Indians, the Spanish settlers in California and the Southwest, and British fur traders in the Northwest.

In this book are the stories of some of the most famous pioneer settlers. John Sutter, a brilliant con man, founded a frontier empire in California. Dedicated missionaries to the Indians, Marcus and Narcissa Whitman also provided shelter and supplies to pioneers on the Oregon Trail in eastern Washington. Brigham Young, the fiery Mormon leader, brought his persecuted followers to Salt Lake

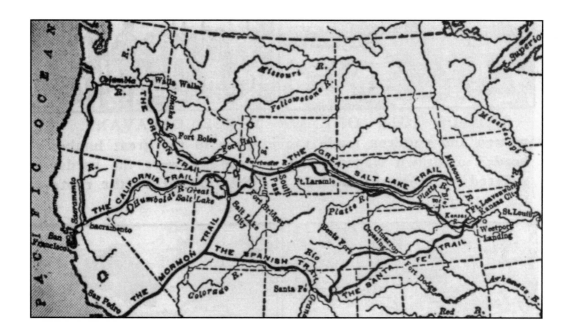

City, Utah. John McLoughlin directed the British Hudson's Bay Company in the Oregon country for 22 years. Founder of the first Catholic missions in Montana and Idaho, Father Peter De Smet, a Jesuit priest, was one of the few white men trusted by the Northwest and Plains Indians.

Some of these brave souls were born in Europe, others in North America or Mexico. Some settled in the West hoping to find riches. Others came to spread the word of God as they understood it. All exhibited strength, courage, and resourcefulness as they explored the land and built missions and towns on the frontier. They remain outstanding examples of the pioneer spirit that made—and still makes—the United States a great nation.

Starting from the Missouri River in Missouri or Nebraska, the trails on this map brought tens of thousands of pioneers west in the 1840s and 1850s. Before that, the trails had been used by mountain men searching for furs and Indians traveling to trade or hunt.

12

Chapter One

Juan de Oñate
and the
Founding of New Mexico

O n April 30, 1598, a caravan of Spanish colonists led by a *conquistador* (Spanish for conqueror) in his forties made camp on the banks of the river we now call the Rio Grande, not far from present-day El Paso, Texas. The conquistador, Juan de Oñate, took formal possession "of all the kingdoms and provinces of New Mexico" for Spain's King Philip II. During the next decade, Oñate would work to establish a Spanish settlement in what is now the state of New Mexico.

Since many records from the sixteenth century have been lost, we know little about the early life of Juan de Oñate (pronounced Oh-NYAH-tay). He was born in about 1552 in the city of Zacatecas in the province of Zacatecas, now a Mexican state. His father, Cristóbal, was governor of Nueva Galicia, a

No portrait was made of Juan de Oñate (c.1552-1626) in his lifetime. But after decades of studying Spanish military uniforms and riding gear from the colonial period, internationally renowned artist José Cisneros has made a series of historical drawings. This is his depiction of Juan de Oñate, published in 1980.

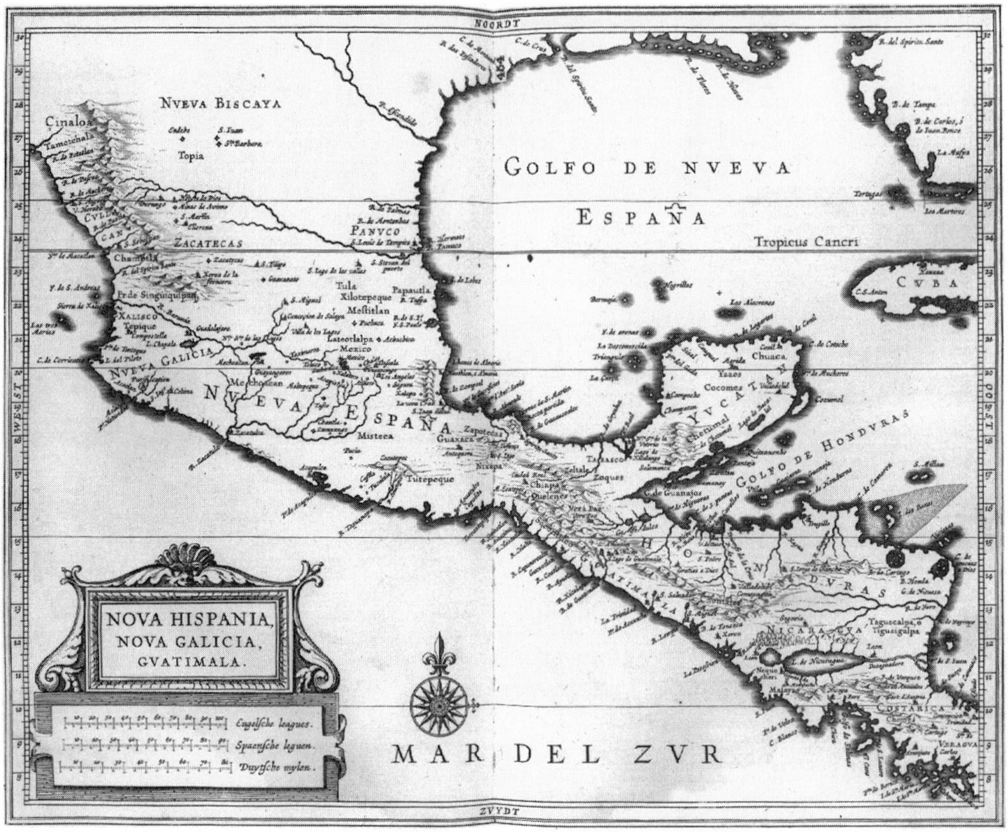
NOORDT
NVEVA BISCAYA
Topia
Cinaloa
ZACATECAS
PANVCO
GOLFO DE NVEVA
ESPAÑA
Tropicus Cancri
CVBA
Tula
Mexico
NVEVA GALICIA
NVEVA ESPAÑA
Misteca
Zapotecas
Tutepeque
Zoques
YVCATAN
Cocomes
Chuaca
GOLFO DE HONDVRAS
NOVA HISPANIA,
NOVA GALICIA,
GVATIMALA.
Engelsche leagues.
Spaensche leguen.
Duytsche mylen.
MAR DEL ZVR
ZVYDT

A 1625 Latin and Spanish map of the Spanish territories of New Spain in what is now Mexico and Central America. The map shows the northern and western provinces of Zacatecas, Nueva Galicia, and Nueva Vizcaya (shown as "Biscaya"). Nueva Vizcaya was then the frontier of New Spain.

region to the southwest. Thanks to the discovery of silver there, he was a wealthy man.

When Juan was growing up, he traveled back and forth with his father between the family estate in Zacatecas and Mexico City, the flourishing capital of New Spain. He probably was educated by Roman Catholic friars who typically tutored the sons of the Spanish *hidalgos*, or noblemen.

By his teens, Juan was battling the Indians in Nueva Galicia, whose war with the Spaniards would last almost 50 years. He led troops into battle and funded military expeditions in his early twenties, preparing himself for a life of colonial work. He also scouted out new silver mines, gaining the wealth he would later use for his New Mexico venture.

In his late thirties, Juan married Isabel Tolosa Cortés Moctezuma, the daughter of one of his father's partners. The couple would have two children. Their son, Cristóbal, was born about 1590, and their daughter, María, in 1598 or 1599.

During these years, King Philip II of Spain was becoming interested in settling the area north of what is now Mexico. In 1593, the king instructed the viceroy (ruler) of New Spain to select a man to lead an expedition. The viceroy decided to establish a Spanish colony in the region north of the river we know as the Rio Grande. The leader had to be wealthy, for he would be funding most of the expedition himself. On September, 21, 1595, after several delays, Oñate's years of loyal service were rewarded with a commission calling for the "exploration, pacification, and conquest of New Mexico." Oñate would be the *adelantado*, or colonial ruler, of the territory he conquered for Spain.

Oñate immediately set about making preparations for the long journey from Zacatecas across the desert lands to the north. Hundreds of adventurers flocked to join his expedition, lured by the chance of finding riches in the fabled Seven Cities of Cibola, believed to be located north of Mexico. Soon, however, preparations were put on hold. Oñate's rivals, envious of his chance to find wealth and power in New Mexico, tried to convince the authorities of New Spain that he was unfit to lead such an important undertaking. Other delays were caused by the

Isabel was a descendant of both Moctezuma (1480?-1520), the famous Aztec emperor (above), and Hernán Cortés, the Spaniard who conquered him.

According to his commission, Oñate received the civilian title of governor and the military rank of captain-general, then the highest rank a man could achieve in the Spanish military service. He was also given the prestigious title *adelantado*, like the conquistadors of old. As adelantado, he had almost unlimited power over both the colonists and the native people of the conquered lands.

Founded by Saint Francis of Assisi in the early thirteenth century, the Franciscans were originally an order of wandering preachers so poor they had to beg for food and shelter. They became effective missionaries on colonial expeditions.

appointment of a new viceroy and disagreements over the expedition contract. Then orders from the king halted the expedition. Finally, in late summer 1597, Oñate was again given the go-ahead.

Due to the delays, Oñate had lost many men and supplies. "The army was dwindling away," complained the expedition's historian, "the priests were leaving." Early the next year, the expedition party was finally ready. Traveling with his eight-year-old son, Cristóbal, Oñate left the staging area near the city of Santa Bárbara in the province of Nueva Vizcaya. This northernmost outpost of New Spain was over 300 miles due south of present-day El Paso, Texas. Although records differ, the party included about 130 soldiers, many of them traveling with families, and 10 Franciscan missionaries. An unknown number of Indians also marched north behind Oñate's banner. Many of the single men took only the clothes on their backs. Richer settlers rode horses fitted with decorated saddles and carried their own weapons. The caravan, with its 80 wagons and 7,000 head of livestock, is said to have stretched for more than four miles as it made its way north.

Oñate had spent time in northern Mexico and knew that water would be scarce as the caravan traveled across the deserts of what is now the state of Chihuahua in Mexico. He sent advance parties to scout for the best trails and find the few water holes between Santa Bárbara and the Rio Grande. But the lack of water was only one of the difficulties faced by the expedition as it traveled north. They were also under constant threat of attack by Indians.

In difficult moments, Oñate rallied his followers "like Julius Caesar," wrote Gaspar Perez de Villagrá, the expedition's historian. "Come, noble soldiers, knights of Christ," the captain-general cried. "Here is presented the finest opportunity for you to show your mettle and courage and to prove that you are deserving of the glories which lie in store for you."

Finally, after journeying for several months, the caravan reached the river the Spanish called Rio del Norte (the Rio Grande). After taking possession of the land in the name of Philip II, Oñate allowed the expeditionaries to rest for a week.

King Philip II (1527-1598) oversaw the great spread of Spanish colonization in the New World.

As this 1625 map detail shows, the Spaniards believed the Pacific Ocean was quite close to the area they were entering (which was just west of Texas). The Pacific, they hoped, could be reached by the Rio del Norte (R. del Norto). The Rio Grande actually runs from Colorado to the Gulf of Mexico.

The members of the expedition were thankful for reaching the river. Both the people and the pack animals were near death from thirst. The Rio Grande provided shady trees, fresh water, and plentiful fish.

A Franciscan priest conducted Mass, and hymns were sung honoring God for granting the expedition success crossing the desert. A group performed a play that had been written by one of the soldiers serving under Oñate. In the play, Indians gratefully received the Roman Catholic faith from the hands of the Franciscan missionaries and Oñate easily overcame any resistance to his conquest of the territory he named New Mexico.

New Mexico before Oñate

The region that is today the state of New Mexico was home to prehistoric Indian peoples long before the first European saw the New World of the Americas. As long as 20,000 years ago, early Indian cultures thrived in the area.

By about 1500 B.C., the region was occupied by people called the Basket-makers, ancestors of the Anasazis and of the Pueblo Indians who still live in New Mexico today. The Pueblos' ancestors made the first North American pottery and the bow and arrow. About 1,000 years ago the Anasazi culture was at its height. The highly advanced people built cities of cliff dwellings and raised crops on irrigated plots. They wove fabric from cotton and made beautiful pottery and jewelry.

By the fifteenth century, the Anasazis had abandoned their cliff dwellings. At the time of the Spanish conquest, the Pueblo and Zuñi (Zuñi-speaking Pueblo) Indians, descendants of the Anasazis, grew corn, beans, and squash in irrigated plots along the Rio Grande. They were peaceful people who clashed only with raiding nomadic hunters of the Apache and Navajo tribes.

It is thought that the first Europeans to visit present-day New Mexico were Álvar Nuñez Cabeza de Vaca and a group of explorers under his command sometime between 1528 and 1536. In the late 1530s, a Franciscan priest and a black slave named Esteban entered the region, searching for the legendary wealth of the Seven Cities of Cibola. The famed conquistador Francisco

Vásquez de Coronado led an expedition to seize these treasures (1540-1542), but he, like several later explorers, failed to find gold. Coronado's brutal murders of Pueblo Indians who resisted supplying food to his party earned lasting Indian hostility for the Spanish.

Another expedition 40 years later renewed the Spanish desires to colonize New Mexico. The leader reported finding precious minerals and fertile pasture lands that could support a permanent colony. By the end of the sixteenth century, Spain was finally ready to colonize New Mexico.

The legend of the Seven Cities of Cibola was inspired by Zuñi pueblos in New Mexico. The real pueblos, however, were disappointingly lacking in gold. Now in ruins, this pueblo, Hawikuh, was probably the one raided by Coronado and his men.

Pueblos are settlements of multi-story buildings constructed by a number of Indian groups, including the Ácomas, Zuñis, and Hopis, who are collectively called Pueblo Indians after their villages.

The trail blazed by Oñate and his followers extended the Camino Real, or Royal Highway, more than 600 miles. From that time on, it ran almost 2,000 miles, from Mexico City to Oñate's settlements in New Mexico.

Soon after they arrived, the Spanish staged a play called "The Moors and the Christians" for chiefs of the local Indian pueblos. It depicted the conquest of the Moors of Spain by the Spanish. In mock battles, soldiers showed off their horsemanship and the power of their weapons. Villagrá said the festivities concluded with a "thunderous discharge of artillery, which caused great fear and wonder among the barbarians."

At the Santo Domingo pueblo, about 35 miles south of their destination, the Spanish finally got to enact the drama in real life. The Spaniards informed the Indians that their land now belonged to the king of Spain. In addition, announced Oñate's men, the Indians must accept the Catholic faith. If they were loyal to King Philip II and served God, the Indians were promised protection from their enemies on earth and everlasting life in Heaven. But any who refused to accept Philip's "generosity" would suffer war. Men, women and children would be killed and villages destroyed. Faced with close to 200 armed soldiers, it was not surprising that the native people submitted to the terrible terms.

On July 11, 1598, Oñate and the others in his expedition reached the pueblos of Okhe and Yunge, near the present-day site of Española, New Mexico, where the Chama River joins the Rio Grande. On the east bank of the Rio Grande they took shelter with the Indians in the Okhe pueblo, which they called San Juan. Within two months, the Spaniards had erected a church in San Juan, but they intended to build a new city nearby.

All was not well in the tiny settlement on the banks of the Rio Grande. Even though they forced the Indians to work for them, life was still hard. Many of the settlers who had come in search of easy wealth were disheartened when they realized that they would have to work long and hard just to scratch out a living in the desolate land of the frontier. Irrigation ditches would have to be dug and crops planted. Some of the noblemen refused to

work. Oñate's harsh military rule also turned settlers against him. A few threatened mutiny or desertion.

Just two months after arriving, four of the settlers fled south for Mexico. Oñate responded like the soldier he was. Immediately, he sent four of his military leaders in hot pursuit with orders that the escapees be executed as soon as they were captured. Two weeks later, the deserters were cornered, and soldiers beheaded two of the offenders. The other two fled into the desert on foot and, no doubt, died there of thirst or exposure.

If Oñate hoped his swift action would put an end to the grumbling in the fledgling settlement, he was sorely disappointed. Unhappiness grew with

The pueblo Oñate took over may have looked something like this multi-story Zuñi pueblo from the late 1800s (without the windows). It is so dry in parts of New Mexico that the Indians have cisterns and pots on their roofs to collect rain water.

every passing day. Still, Oñate was determined to make San Juan a success. He sent out scouting parties to find land suitable for farming and ranching. He also came up with a plan to capture buffalo and raise them like cattle. In mid-September 1598, he sent an expedition of 60 men, led by his nephew Vicente de Zaldívar, into the plains east of San Juan. They were ordered to drive a herd of buffalo to the settlement. But the expedition returned without any animals. The buffalo, Zaldívar reported, were too wild and dangerous to control.

While Zaldívar was chasing after the buffalo, Oñate led a party southwest of San Juan. He sought what the Spanish called the South Sea, the vast body of water west of American shores. Geographers of the day believed the Pacific was much closer to the Rio Grande than it actually is. Oñate hoped to find the fabled Pearl Fisheries and trace a water route for New Mexico to use for trade with Spain.

A group of 30 Spanish soldiers and settlers under the leadership of Juan de Zaldívar, Vicente's brother, departed from San Juan to join their leader on his way west. On December 1, Juan de Zaldívar and his men reached the Ácoma pueblo on the top of a mesa reaching more than 350 feet into the sky. Unknown to the Spaniards, the Ácoma Indians had decided to rise against the Spanish and drive them from their lands. When the soldiers, led by Juan de Zaldívar, climbed to the mesa's top, they were attacked by the Indians. Juan and 10 of the men in the party were killed. The survivors raced back to San Juan to spread the alarm.

Along the coast of the South Sea (now the Pacific Ocean and the Gulf of California) were the rumored Pearl Fisheries, full of oysters containing huge pearls for the taking.

The coming of winter and Juan de Zaldívar's unexplained absence made Oñate turn back to San Juan, so he learned of the incident. His response to the Ácoma rebellion was fast and deadly. After a council of war in which the missionaries gave their blessing to what the Spanish considered a just war, Oñate sent 72 men to the Ácoma pueblo. Vicente de Zaldívar, their leader, was determined to avenge his brother's death. He came up with a plan to reach the mesa's seemingly unassailable top. While most of the men attacked up the main path, a smaller group sneaked around the other side of the mesa and scaled the cliff. Once on top, they surprised the Ácomans and were able to defend their position, allowing all the soldiers to ascend. The Ácomans' bows and arrows were no match for Spanish firepower. In the terrible three-day battle, Ácoma men, women, and children were put to the sword. Rather than sur-

The Ácoma pueblo, high atop a sheer mesa, was easily defensible. Indians had lived in this place called Sky City for two centuries.

Before the Spanish soldiers went to do battle with the Indians of the Ácoma pueblo, they confessed their sins to the priests in San Juan and received Communion so that they would go to Heaven if they fell in battle.

render, hundreds hanged themselves or leaped from the mesa to their deaths. Others turned their weapons on each other to deny the Spaniards the satisfaction of killing them.

When the fighting ended, about 500 Ácoma Indians remained alive. The Spanish put the survivors on trial for their attempt to revolt against Spanish authority. Not surprisingly, all were found guilty. In mid-February of 1599, sentences were handed down. All men over the age of 25 had one foot chopped off and were forced into slavery for the Spanish for 20 years. Males between the ages of 12 and 25 and women over the age of 12 escaped the mutilation, but they also were sentenced to 20 years of service to the Spanish. The Ácoma children were sent to Mexico City to be raised as Christians.

While the Spaniards' actions were horrible, Oñate and the others believed they were justified. But the Pueblo Indians resented the Spaniards' violence and their demands for food and labor. Minor outbreaks occurred in the next few years. Each was put down brutally by Oñate and his men.

At some point in 1599 or 1600, the Spaniards decided to take over the Yunge pueblo instead of building a new town by San Juan. The Indians at Yunge were forced to move across the river to San Juan. Oñate renamed the Yunge pueblo San Gabriel, and the Spaniards built a church and remodeled the dwellings in the coming months.

Oñate soon turned his attention to obtaining more soldiers and settlers for San Gabriel. In a letter to the viceroy, Oñate praised New Mexico as a

Within a few years, most of the Ácoma Indians had escaped servitude and rebuilt their pueblo. Ácoma has been continuously occupied to this day.

place where crops could be successfully raised and revenues earned for the Spanish Crown. Convinced, the viceroy authorized an additional 73 soldiers, 6 Franciscan missionaries, and more supplies of food and livestock to be sent to the settlement.

Once the new soldiers arrived at San Gabriel, Oñate was ready once again to try to make New Mexico profitable. He decided to go in search of what the Spanish called the "Quivira"—a fabled city peopled by giants with gold so plentiful that it was used to pave the streets. In June 1601, leading over 70 men with six wagons and about 700 head of live-stock, Oñate headed northeast to find this legendary city. Like other Spanish adventurers who had pre-ceded him into the Great Plains in search of riches, however, he was doomed to failure.

Meanwhile, the settlement Oñate had founded fell on hard times. Many of the settlers were tired of the harsh conditions and scarcity of food on the New Mexican frontier. Now, with Oñate gone, almost all of them scurried south to Mexico. All but one of the Franciscans also abandoned San Gabriel, con-vinced that the Spaniards' treatment of the Indians had ruined any chance of converting them. In late November 1601, Oñate returned empty-handed from his expedition, which had gone as far as pre-sent-day Arkansas City, Kansas. He found San Gabriel almost empty. Only 25 soldiers remained, along with their families and a couple officials.

Oñate knew the abandonment of San Gabriel spelled disaster not just for the colony, but also for himself. The colonists would submit unfavorable

This statue of the Virgin Mary, which stands in the cathedral in Santa Fe, is also called "La Conquistadora." She is the patroness of the conquistadors who conquered the New World.

reports to the viceroy about his activities. As he feared, the settlers did indeed complain bitterly, and the viceroy believed their complaints.

For a time, Oñate was able to delay what he knew would be his eventual recall to Mexico in disgrace. In October 1604, in an effort to prove his own worth and the value of his colony, he led another expedition of 30 soldiers southwest in search of the Pearl Fisheries on the shores of the Pacific Ocean. Four years before, a party under Vicente de Zaldívar had been forced by hostile Indians to turn back without reaching the South Sea. But this expedition did finally make its way to the Gulf of California in January 1605. Oñate, however, was disappointed. The Pearl Fisheries, like Quivira, were a myth. And the Gulf of California was just too far from the settlement in New Mexico to serve as a trade route to Mexico.

By 1608, the authorities in New Spain were tired of Oñate's failed attempts to find riches in New Mexico. The government's portion of the cost was simply too great at a time when the once all-powerful Spanish empire was shrinking. A new viceroy,

On his way back from his trip to the South Sea in 1605, Oñate stopped at what is now called Inscription Rock at El Morro National Monument in New Mexico. There he carved this message still visible in the soft stone. It reads in old Spanish, "There passed this way the Adelantado Don Juan de Oñate, from the discovery of the South Sea, on the 16th of April, 1605."

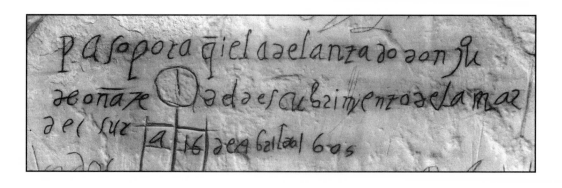

appointed at about that time, recommended that the settlement be continued only for missionary purposes. Oñate, added the viceroy, should be replaced.

On August 24, 1607, even before he knew he had been recalled, Oñate offered his resignation in an effort to save face. The new viceroy accepted, but he ordered Oñate to remain in New Mexico until a decision was reached about the colony's fate. While the former adelantado waited, he oversaw a historic move. As early as 1607, the remaining colonists began relocating from San Gabriel to an unoccupied valley about 20 miles to the south. This tiny settlement would become Santa Fe.

The wheels of government moved slowly in those days, so several years passed before Oñate was formally accused of 30 charges of mismanagement of his colony and mistreatment of the Indians. In 1614, the *Audiencia*, the judicial authority in Mexico City, found him guilty of 12 of those charges. While he could have been put to death or imprisoned, Oñate was given a relatively light sentence. He was banished from New Mexico forever and ordered not to enter Mexico City for four years. He was also given a stiff fine and stripped of his prestigious titles.

His reputation damaged almost beyond repair, Oñate traveled to Spain for the first time in his life in 1621. For the next several years, he sought a pardon from the Spanish Crown. Finally, in 1623, King Philip IV did at least reimburse his fine.

The former adelantado of New Mexico never returned to the New World. Instead, in 1624, Oñate was granted a royal appointment to inspect mines in

Spain. He collapsed and died on June 3, 1626, at the age of about 74, while inspecting a mine.

While Oñate's time in the New World ended in shame and the settlement he founded was virtually abandoned before he was removed from office, New Mexico did survive. The governor who eventually replaced him—Pedro de Peralta—completed the move to Santa Fe, or "Holy Faith." Officially founded in 1610, Santa Fe is now the capital of the state of New Mexico.

Juan de Oñate had hoped that his son, Cristóbal, would replace him as adelantado. But he was disappointed in this as well. Cristóbal remained in Mexico and took up the family business of mining.

New Mexico from Spanish Rule to Statehood

Even after Pedro de Peralta moved the capital of New Mexico to Santa Fe, colonization was slow. Under Spanish colonial rule, and later as part of Mexico, New Mexico remained a region of cattle and sheep ranches, with mission settlements and a few villages scattered along the Rio Grande.

Spanish brutality kept the Indians quiet for a time after Ácoma's uprising, but there were revolts in the 1640s. Then, in 1680, the San Juan pueblo—the first occupied by Juan de Oñate—rebelled. Led by a medicine man, the Pueblos killed over 400 Spaniards, driving them from New Mexico.

The Palace of the Governors, the residence of the Spanish governors in old Santa Fe, is now a museum.

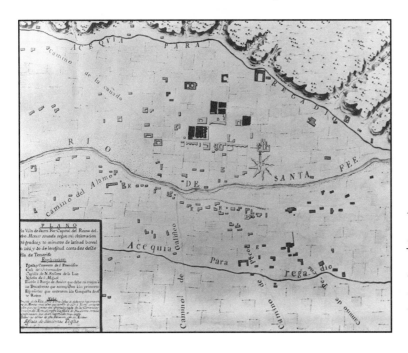

A plan of Santa Fe in 1766, more than 150 years after its founding. Galisteo Street (Camino de Galisteo) and the Old Pecos Trail (Camino de Pecos) are still major thoroughfares in the city.

Just 12 years later, the Spanish retook the territory. Slowly, Spanish ranches, farms, and mines spread in New Mexico.

After Mexico gained its independence from Spain in 1821, New Mexico became a province of Mexico. Contact with the United States began to increase after that time. Traders from Kansas and Missouri realized there were opportunities for profits in New Mexico. By 1822, they had opened the Santa Fe Trail, linking New Mexico with Independence, Missouri.

In 1846, when the United States and Mexico were at war over the lands histori-cally owned by Mexico, New Mexico was occupied by American forces. The region was ceded to the U.S. under the terms of the peace treaty that ended that war. The Territory of New Mexico was officially formed in 1850 and enlarged by the Gadsden Purchase in 1853.

New Mexico remained a wild frontier for several more decades. Conflicts with Indians continued, and ranchers battled it out with farmers over rights to the land. On January 6, 1912, however, New Mexico finally entered the Union as the 47th state, and Santa Fe was named the state capital.

Chapter Two

Eusebio Kino
and the
Missions of Arizona

S ometime in 1663, an 18-year-old university student lay near death in a sickbed in the city of Hala, not far from Innsbruck in present-day Austria. Although his doctors were using the best medicine then available, they had given up hope for his recovery.

One day, a Jesuit priest, whose name is not known to us, came to the young student's sickroom. He talked softly with the student. Turn your life over to God, he suggested. Then maybe you will recover. Eusebio Kino, for that was the young man's name, made a vow to his patron saint, Francis Xavier. He promised that if his life was spared, he would become a Jesuit priest and devote his life to missionary work. When Eusebio recovered from his illness, he did not forget his vow.

This sculpture of Eusebio Francisco Kino (1645-1711) stands in Statuary Hall in the U.S. Capitol. The missionary and explorer wears a crucifix and carries an astrolabe, an instrument used by mapmakers to determine latitude.

Eusebio Kino was born in what was then part of Austria but is now part of Italy. His hometown of Segno is in the beautiful mountainous region known as the Tyrol. The exact date of his birth is not known, but it is believed to be August 10, 1645, because a baptismal record shows that he was christened on that date. Since many infants died soon after birth in those days, it was not unusual for babies to be baptized immediately.

We know little about Eusebio's early life. His father, Franciscus, and his mother, Margherita, were relatively well-off landowners. But since Segno was a village of hard-working farmers, Eusebio probably spent many hours in the fields as a boy.

At the age of about 15, Eusebio left his home village and made his way down a winding mountain path to the city of Trent, where he enrolled in a Jesuit college. It appears that he began to consider becoming a member of the Society of Jesus while he was at Trent. He may have gotten the idea from stories he heard about a relative, Father Martin Martini, who had won fame as a missionary in China.

St. Francis Xavier, known as the "Apostle of the Indies," was born in 1506. One of the first initiates into the Society of Jesus under Ignatius of Loyola, Francis Xavier became a missionary to India in 1542, eventually converting thousands of people throughout the Far East. He died in 1552 and was canonized (made a saint in the Roman Catholic Church) in 1622.

By 1663, Eusebio was a student at the Jesuit college in Hala, a small city in the Tyrolian Alps. It was at this time that he fell ill and made his solemn promise to Saint Francis Xavier.

After completing his studies at Hala, Eusebio made good on his vow and entered the Jesuit order in 1665. For two years, he remained at Hala as what is known as a "novice," studying the Catholic faith in more detail and proving the seriousness of his decision to become a priest.

Jesuits then, and still today, underwent at least 12 years of rigorous training before becoming priests. For 3 years following the completion of his novitiate, Kino studied philosophy at the great Jesuit university of Ingolstadt, in what is now southern Germany. In 1670, he returned to Hala as a student teacher. This period of his training lasted until 1673, at which time he returned to Ingolstadt, where he spent four more years studying theology.

Kino displayed remarkable ability in the field of mathematics. In 1676, while he was at Ingolstadt, he was given the chance to become a professor of mathematics at the university. Kino turned down the prestigious offer, however, remembering his vow to become a missionary.

After he finished his training in 1677, Kino continued teaching at Ingolstadt. But he wrote letter after letter to the Father General of the Jesuits (the order's earthly leader), volunteering to go abroad as a missionary. As a good Jesuit who had taken a vow of obedience, he would go wherever he was sent, but he had long dreamed of following in the footsteps of Father Martini, his relative who had gone to the Far East, and his patron saint, Francis Xavier. Finally, in 1678, Kino received word he was being sent abroad as a missionary.

Two missionaries—Kino and Father Antonio Kerschpamer—were being sent to foreign missions. However, one was to go to the Philippines and one to Mexico. It was left up to the two Jesuits to decide who would go where. Since neither wanted to be selfish and choose first, they could not make up their

People use the term novice now for a beginner at any activity. Novices had to complete a novitiate, a period of training, before they could be ordained as priests.

St. Ignatius of Loyola (1491-1556) founded the Society of Jesus, commonly known as the Jesuit order, in about 1540. Jesuits, following their founder's wishes, are dedicated to teaching and missionary work.

minds. Finally, they came up with a solution. "While we were engaged in this pious argument," Kino wrote to a friend, "it occurred to us to settle our devout quarrel by lots." They tore two slips of paper. On one was written "Mexico." On the other, "Philippines." Father Antonio chose first. When he unfolded his paper and read the word "Philippines," Kino's dream of going to the Orient was at an end. But the young priest accepted the outcome as God's will.

On January 27, 1681, after more than two years of preparation and one delay after another, Kino and another Jesuit, Father Adam Gerstl, set sail together. The difficult voyage across the Atlantic Ocean took the ship from the Spanish city of Cádiz to Vera Cruz (now Veracruz) on the east coast of Mexico. The ship dropped anchor in Vera Cruz harbor in early May after 96 days at sea.

Kino and Father Gerstl quickly set out from Vera Cruz, riding mules across the land the Spanish called "Tierra Caliente" (the hot land). They climbed the steep slopes of "Tierra Templada" (the temperate, or mild, land) and into the high country, called "Tierra Fria" (the cold land). On their mules, the Jesuits rode first to Puebla de los Angeles, about halfway between Vera Cruz and Mexico City. There the Jesuits had already established a school and a church that one earlier visitor said "surpassed in beauty and amount of gold anything I have ever seen in Germany." From Puebla de los Angeles, they then traveled further northwest to Mexico City, where they arrived in early June.

At the time of Kino's arrival, Isidro Atondo y Antillón, a former governor of Mexico, was preparing an expedition from Mexico City to what is today the peninsula south of California known as Baja California. His goals were to explore the region and establish missions. Father Kino was chosen as one of the missionaries to California.

As Kino waited for the Atondo expedition to leave Mexico City, he wrote and published a pamphlet about a comet that had appeared in 1680. This little book proved his skill as a mathematician. After its publication, he was named the royal cosmographer for the Atondo expedition. This meant he was to be its mapmaker, astronomer, and surveyor, as well as a missionary priest.

This map shows Mexico City and the surrounding area in 1618. When Kino arrived in 1681, the city was much bigger and grander. One missionary writing about Mexico City at that time claimed, "In the city there is so much gold and silver that the interiors of the churches are magnificently adorned with it."

This portion of a 1717 map shows how short the distance was between the Mexican mainland by the Sinaloa River (Cinaloa) and La Paz near the tip of Baja California—about 150 miles. Today a ferry runs regularly between La Paz and a point near the Sinaloa River.

By March 1682, Kino was in Pueblo de Nío on the Sinaloa River, just across the Gulf of California from Baja California. After a delay of almost a full year, the expedition finally set sail on January 17, 1683. The group made many stops along the way, so it took more than two months to reach the port of La Paz, which was on the Bay of Peace at the southern end of Baja California. On April 2, Kino and the others disembarked and came ashore. Atondo claimed the land for the Spanish king, Charles II, and Kino raised a cross for the Roman Catholic Church. Within days, the party had erected a small fort with a log church and a few huts.

At first, the Indians living near Santísima Trinidad (Holy Trinity), as the Spaniards named the settlement, were friendly. Within just a few months, however, a state of war existed between the natives and the Europeans on the shores of the Bay of Peace. Short of supplies and fearing an Indian attack, Atondo's party fled the area in mid-July.

For the next three years, Kino frequently made the 150-mile voyage between the Mexican mainland and the Baja Peninsula, trying to establish missions and win the trust of the Indians of Baja California. He learned the Indians' language and taught Spanish to young Indians. In this way, he gained some converts to the Catholic faith. He also explored and mapped what was then a little-known frontier. Kino's work in Baja California ended in 1686, when the Spanish government decided to suspend the Baja California missions due to a lack of funds.

Kino soon got permission to go to what is now northern Mexico, to work with the Guaymas and Seri Indians. He traveled north, arriving in Sonora, Mexico, in late February 1687. His superiors there ordered him to proceed to an unexplored region then known as Pimería Alta. This region included what is now the northern half of the Mexican state of Sonora and part of the southern half of present-day Arizona. It extended from the San Ignacio River on the south to the Gila River in the north and from the San Pedro River on the east to the Gulf of California and the Colorado River in the west. It was in this region that Kino was to spend almost a quarter century as a missionary priest.

"[Kino's] conversation was of the . . . names of Jesus and Mary, and of the [Indians] for whom he was forever offering prayers to God."
—a fellow Jesuit

Kino relished the hardships of the frontier. He even tried to make it more difficult, another Jesuit remembered, for "he always took his food without salt, and with mixtures of herbs which made it more distasteful."

Arizona before Eusebio Kino

It is believed that the first Indian inhabitants of the region we know as Arizona migrated to the area some time between 10,000 and 25,000 years ago. By about 4,000 years ago, these hunter-gatherers had become farmers, and corn, squash, beans, and cotton became their main crops over time. The Indians constructed sophisticated irrigation systems, diverting rivers to provide water to fields in arid areas.

The two main Indian cultures in early Arizona were the Hohokams and the Anasazis. By the time Europeans first visited the New World, these cultures had evolved into the Pimas and Pueblos. The Hopi Pueblos lived in northeast Arizona. The Pimas and the Yumas were in the southern and western parts of the region. Navajos and Apaches had also migrated into the eastern part of the state.

The first European to see Arizona was probably the Spaniard Francisco Vásquez de Coronado, who explored the region from 1540 to 1542. Coronado was searching for the famed Seven Cities of Cibola. In the course of explorations, Coronado's expedition discovered the Grand Canyon of the Colorado River. Several more Spanish explorers and missionaries came to Arizona in the next century and a half.

Francisco Vásquez de Coronado (c.1510-1554) and his men failed to find gold in North America, but their explorations, ranging from Texas and Kansas to Arizona, opened trails to the Southwest from Mexico.

In Kino's time, the Pimería Alta was home to two major Indian groups: the Pima Nation (including the Sobaípuris and the Papagos) and the Yumas. They were, for the most part, peaceful people, farmers who raised cotton, corn, beans, melons, gourds, and wheat. Their culture was centuries old, and, when Kino arrived in Pimería Alta, evidence of its former greatness was visible in the form of the ruins of cities and the remains of miles of aqueducts used to irrigate crops and provide water.

In early 1687, soon after his arrival in Pimería Alta, Kino made his way north to an Indian village called Cosari. Cosari was on the banks of the San Miguel River about 50 miles south of the United States border in present-day Sonora, Mexico. There he founded the mission of Nuestra Señora de los Dolores (Our Lady of Sorrows).

On a promontory overlooking the San Miguel and the fertile lands along the riverbank, Kino, with help from Indian workers, soon built a small chapel and a tiny house for himself. The natives, Kino wrote, worked, "with very great pleasure and with all willingness." They made "adobes, doors, windows, etc., for a very good house and church to replace the temporary structures." In six years, the mission church was finally ready for a formal dedication. No sign of the mission is visible today, but for 25 years it served as Kino's home and headquarters as he explored and started missions in southern Arizona.

In the years from 1687 to 1711, Father Kino traveled far and wide throughout northern Sonora and southern Arizona. For the first six years, he was

The Pimas call themselves the O'odham, or desert people.

Kino chose the site for Dolores because it was near a Pima village whose chief, Coxi, also ruled over a number of villages to the west. Kino soon baptized two of Coxi's sons, a sure sign that he would have success as a missionary in the region.

the only European in the region. In a quarter century, the priest started several missions in Arizona. He founded San Gabriel de Guebavi, not far from modern Nogales, and San José de Tumacacori, between Tucson and Nogales, in 1691. The next year, he founded the famous mission San Xavier del Bac on the banks of the Santa Cruz River about seven miles south of present-day Tucson. San Xavier del Bac later became the central Spanish mission in Arizona.

Virtually all the labor to found the missions was performed by Pima Indian converts called neophytes. Not only did they build the churches, but they also worked ranches and planted orchards and crops. Some ran water-powered flour mills, and others became skilled carpenters and blacksmiths.

The mission building took decades. The San Xavier church was not completed for more than a half century, and the current church at Tumacacori

The ruin of the mission church at San Gabriel de Guebavi may date from Kino's time. As at all the missions, Kino started a ranch at Guebavi to support the Indian workers.

This beautiful church now stands at the San Xavier del Bac Mission. Kino was "received with all affection" by the Sobaípuri Indians there, and he educated them in geography and history as well as in the Roman Catholic faith.

was not begun until 1800. Kino never saw the completed churches that we are able to view today.

The missions were the first outposts of European civilization on the frontier of Arizona. They provided sanctuaries for Pimas who were often raided by the hostile Apaches of the region. In addition, they were self-sufficient communities. Mission Dolores, the largest of the missions, had a ranch where cattle, sheep, horses, oxen, and mules were raised, as well as orchards rich with fig, pomegranate, pear, and peach trees; wheat and corn fields; and a water-powered mill for grinding grain.

All told, Father Kino founded 25 missions in Pimería Alta, including the 3 in present-day Arizona. In addition, he established 73 *visitas*, which were

Constantly on the road, Kino's bed "consisted of two calf-skins for mattresses, two blankets such as the Indians use for covers, and a pack saddle for a pillow."

"No one ever saw in [Kino] any vice whatsoever, for the discovery of lands and the conversion of souls had purified him. These, then, are the virtues of Father Kino: he prayed much, and was considered as without vice. He neither smoked nor took snuff; nor wine, nor slept in a bed. . . . He never had more than two coarse shirts, because he gave everything as alms to the Indians. He was merciful to others, but cruel to himself."
—a fellow Jesuit

small missions that were visited by priests because they did not have resident priests. It is impossible to know how many Pimas and others were baptized by Kino, but the number was surely in the thousands. Kino treated the Indians with kindness, often protecting them from intolerant Spanish officials.

While the Indians' devotion to Kino was great, they mistrusted other Europeans. In 1695, some of the Pimas revolted, killing at least one Jesuit. But when the Indians came to Mission Dolores, they did not lift a hand against Kino. He was soon back at his work, moving among the natives without fear.

Kino's endurance was remarkable. At the age of 51, he made a 1,500-mile journey on horseback from Dolores to Mexico City in 53 days, including stops to say Mass and meet with other Jesuits. Kino was 56 when he heard on May 3, 1700, that an Indian was to be executed in Sonora the next day. He hopped on his horse and rode all through the night to save the man's life.

Kino had a particular fondness for Indian children. Often, as he rode around the mission grounds, he was followed by groups of children, all clamoring for his attention. In his diary, Kino recorded a story of how one young boy who was living at the mission resisted the efforts of his parents to take him away, calling for help from "Padre Eusebio."

Devoted to the people of the Pimería Alta, Kino refused a chance to go to Baja California to establish mission settlements in the 1690s. To support the new missions, however, he shipped cattle and supplies to the peninsula. Convinced that Baja

California was a peninsula and not, as was widely believed, a large island, Kino also began to dream of opening a road from Mexico to Baja California so that supplies could be shipped without having to make the water passage across the Gulf of California. This dream, however, was not realized in his lifetime.

On his trips to Baja California, Kino explored and mapped the uncharted territory west of Pimería Alta. Finally, he was able to prove that, in his triumphant words, "California is not an island, but rather a peninsula!" How did he resolve the old

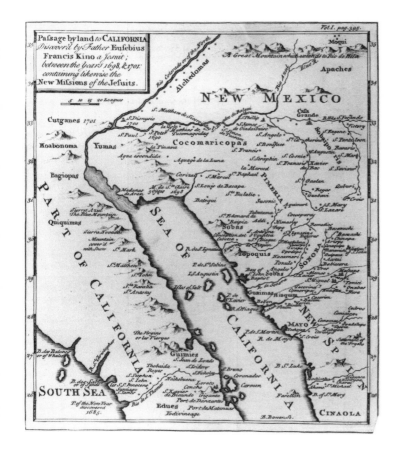

Kino's 1702 map of Baja California

debate among mapmakers? Kino managed to reach California in a long trip overland in 1702.

Throughout his life, Kino's great joy was always his work with the Indians. Even when he was forced to curtail his explorations as he grew older, he continued serving his missions, riding hundreds of miles in some months to oversee the cattle ranches and the planting and harvesting of crops.

In March 1711, Kino was at the mission at Magdalena, not far from Dolores, to dedicate a new chapel to Francis Xavier, his patron saint. While he was there, the 65-year-old priest collapsed and died on March 15, 1711.

"Father Kino died in the year 1711, having spent twenty-four years in glorious labor in this Pimería. . . . He died as he had lived, with extreme poverty and humility."
—Father Luís Velarde, describing Kino's death

Arizona after Kino

In 1767, a half century after Kino's death, Jesuits were banished from Arizona by the Spanish king, who suspected disloyalty. In their place, Spaniard Juan Bautista de Anza and the Franciscan priest F. T. H. Garcés founded missions among the Yumas in southwest Arizona.

In 1821, Mexico won independence from Spain. But American trappers and traders soon made their way into what was now Mexican Arizona. The Americans wanted the United States, not Mexico, to have jurisdiction over the land.

Finally, the two nations went to war over a vast amount of territory. In 1848,

Juan Bautista de Anza (1735-1788) opened Kino's dreamed-of road from Sonora, Mexico, through Arizona to Monterey, California, in 1774.

Mexico lost the Mexican War—a war it refers to as "the Great North American Intervention." The United States obtained the area of Arizona lying north of the Gila River, making it part of the New Mexico Territory. The region that Kino had settled south of the Gila was made part of the territory in 1853 with the Gadsden Purchase.

On February 24, 1863, President Abraham Lincoln signed the law that made Arizona a separate territory, and settlement increased. By the end of the 1860s, the U.S. Army had built several forts in the region. During the remainder of the nineteenth century, the territory's population grew rapidly, especially after Apache resistance was quashed in 1886. Large cattle ranches were established, and silver and copper mining became major industries. The late 1800s saw the founding of several Mormon settlements and the construction of railroad lines to California.

As the territory's population grew, thanks to irrigation projects that made agriculture possible in areas that had been arid, many residents desired statehood. On February 14, 1912, Arizona was admitted to the Union as the 48th state.

American troops enter Mexico City in triumph in September 1847. The Treaty of Guadalupe Hidalgo, signed in February 1848, transferred most of Arizona and New Mexico, parts of Texas, Colorado, and Wyoming, and all of Utah, Nevada, and California to the United States.

Chapter Three

Junípero Serra
and
Spanish California

On July 16, 1769, a 55-year-old Catholic priest named Junípero Serra celebrated Mass on a hillside overlooking the Pacific Ocean. Father Serra was a small, frail man, only two or three inches taller than five feet. He walked with a limp and had to struggle to catch his breath. Serra was a Franciscan, a member of the religious order founded by Saint Francis of Assisi in 1209, and a missionary in what the Spanish called Alta, or upper, California. The empty hillside where he celebrated Mass on that summer day about 230 years ago had just been christened Mission San Diego. The city we know today as San Diego, California, would sprout around that site.

The third child of Antonio and Margarita Serra, Junípero Serra was born at one o'clock in the

Junípero Serra (1713-1784) was universally loved by the priests who worked under him. One of them, Francisco Palóu, wrote Serra's biography to inspire others "to follow in his glorious footsteps . . . until there shall not remain in this immense region . . . a single unbeliever."

morning on November 24, 1713, in a small stone house in the village of Petra on Majorca, an island in the Mediterranean Sea off the coast of Spain. Later that morning, the new baby was rushed to the nearby Church of San Pedro, where he was baptized and christened Miguel José. The Serras' first two babies had not survived, and they were taking no chances their new son would die without being baptized.

Even as a boy, Miguel was attracted to the religious life. He frequently visited the gray-robed Franciscans at the Convent of San Bernadino near his home. (A convent, in those days, was the name given to a community of monks as well as nuns.)

In 1717, when Serra was four years old, vast amounts of North and Central America were claimed by Spain. In addition to California, New Mexico, and Mexico, a Florida that stretched over the entire southeast was Spanish.

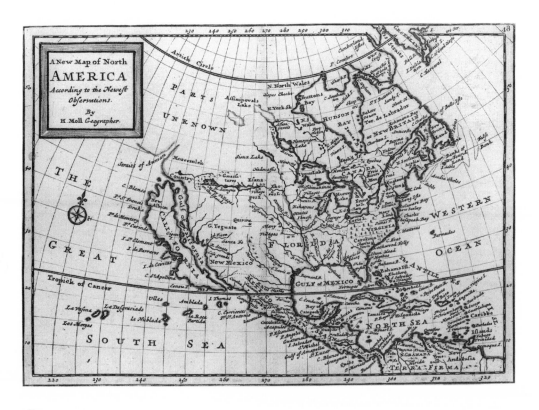

Much of his free time was spent praying in the convent's 13 chapels, each of which was dedicated to a different martyr who had died for the faith.

On September 14, 1730, at the age of just 16, Miguel joined the Franciscan order at the Convent of Jesus in Palma, the capital of Majorca. He made his religious vows of poverty, chastity, and obedience a year later. When he joined the order, he took the name Junípero (pronounced Hoo-NEE-pay-ro). That was the name of the joyful and faithful companion of St. Francis of Assisi.

In preparation for the priesthood, Junípero studied for the next seven years. He was ordained in 1737. A brilliant student, Serra was soon chosen to be the new lector (teacher) in philosophy at the University of Palma, famous for its scholarship.

For nine years, Serra taught philosophy and theology at the university. He won renown as both a teacher and preacher, but Serra wanted to do more. In 1748, when he learned that the Apostolic College of San Fernando in Mexico City—a university established to train missionaries for work among the Indians of the New World—was seeking missionaries, Serra answered the call.

In April 1749, after paying a last visit to his younger sister, Juana, and his parents, Serra left Palma with Francisco Palóu, a friend and former student. From Palma, the priests made their way to Cádiz on the southern coast of Spain, where they boarded a vessel that would carry them to Vera Cruz in Mexico. On August 30, Serra, Palóu, and Juan Crespí, another former student, set sail for the New

"I was always rather sickly and very small of body . . . but after making the vows I began to grow in strength and health and succeeded in reaching a medium stature . . . for which I ever give thanks to God."
—Junípero Serra

A fellow Franciscan said Serra's words were "worthy of being printed in letters of gold."

"I want to ask you again to do me the favor of consoling my parents, who, I know, are going through a great sorrow," wrote Serra to his cousin on August 20, 1749. "Nothing else but the love of God has led me to leave them."

World with other Franciscan missionaries. Their somewhat rickety old ship was caught in a fierce storm off the coast of Mexico. In a letter to his cousin, Serra said it was a miracle that they reached Vera Cruz safely.

While the rest of the missionaries rode west from Vera Cruz to Mexico City on horseback, Serra and one other Franciscan made their way on foot. The two Franciscans chose to follow the example of St. Francis of Assisi for their 200-mile journey. They carried no food and begged as they trudged along the narrow trail known as Camino Real. For 18 days, they walked under the scorching sun across the Sierra Madre Oriental and into the central Mexican plateau. Sleeping under the stars most nights, Serra lay on his back, clutching a large cross to his chest.

Strange things happened on this journey. Once, when Serra and his companion were tired and thirsty, a man on horseback appeared. He gave each priest an incredibly delicious pomegranate that renewed their energy. A few days later, they were given a loaf of bread by a friendly farmer, but they gave it away to a starving beggar. That evening, as the priests lay exhausted and hungry by the side of the trail, another horseman appeared. He handed the two men a small, foul-smelling loaf of bread. Despite its smell, the bread tasted wonderful and was unbelievably rejuvenating. Serra later told Palóu he believed their mysterious provider might have been St. Joseph, the earthly father of Jesus.

Born in about 1181, St. Francis was the son of a wealthy merchant in the town of Assisi, Italy. Francis began preaching in his early twenties and founded his Roman Catholic order a few years later. The most important principles of the order were poverty, charity, humility, and a love of nature.

Even with the miraculous aid, the journey was difficult. Near the end of the trek, Serra was bitten on the left foot by an insect. His left leg swelled and he could hardly stand. By the time he limped into Mexico City on January 1, 1750, his foot and leg were covered with open sores. His leg never completely healed and pained him for the rest of his life.

Soon after his arrival at the apostolic college, Serra was sent to work with the Pame Indians in the Sierra Gorda region of Mexico, about 150 miles northeast of Mexico City. For more than eight years, he worked tirelessly in the missions of the Sierra Gorda. He became the director of the five missions in the region and oversaw the construction of new churches. In contrast to most Spanish authorities, Serra used gentleness and persuasion to gain converts and convince the Indians to become farmers and ranchers instead of nomadic hunters.

Serra was recalled to Mexico City in 1758, and he spent the next nine years there. For six months of each year, he oversaw novice Franciscans at the apostolic college and directed the choir. The rest of the year was spent as a traveling preacher.

In the Franciscan way, Serra ate very little and limited his sleep to about four hours a night. He prayed the rest of the night and practiced what was known as "mortification" of his flesh. This meant he lashed himself with a whip or beat his chest with a stone to atone for sinful thoughts. Despite his bad leg and a shortness of breath that might have been asthma, Serra walked more than 5,500 miles in those years as a traveling priest.

Serra himself helped build the churches and other structures of his Sierra Gorda missions, and he painstakingly designed every detail of the buildings.

In July 1767, Serra was appointed to lead a group of missionaries to Baja (lower) California to take the place of Jesuit priests who had been expelled from missions there after falling into disfavor with King Charles III of Spain. For almost a year, Serra, Palóu, and a group of Franciscans maintained the missions. Then, in mid-1768, the inspector general of New Spain, José de Gálvez, arrived in Baja California and announced his intention to occupy Alta (upper) California. Gálvez soon chose Serra to accompany him as a missionary.

The journey to Alta California the next year took a terrible toll on Serra. At the end of the first day's riding, his leg was so swollen and painful that he was unable to stand except to say Mass. Gaspar de Portolá, the party's commander, offered to have him brought back to Baja California, but Serra refused. For two days, he was carried. When he saw one of the mule drivers applying poultices to a mule's sore leg, Serra asked the man to do the same for him. The driver packed a mixture of hot tallow and herbs on Serra's leg. Soon, the priest was able to walk and ride with little pain.

Reaching San Diego Bay on July 1, 1769, Serra and the others met two ships and another overland party. Many Spaniards and Indians on the expedition had already perished on the way from diseases, but the mission work had to go on. On July 16, about two weeks after the bedraggled party arrived in San Diego, Serra founded Mission San Diego. The mission's start was not promising. In addition to supply shortages, the local Indians were hostile.

In 1767, King Charles III of Spain ordered Jesuits to leave New Spain because he feared they planned to challenge his claim to the throne.

"I trust that God will give me the strength to reach San Diego, as He has given me the strength to come so far. In case He does not, I will confirm myself to His most holy will. Even though I should die on the way, *I shall not turn back.*"
—Serra to Portolá

Serra was delighted with the land he found around San Diego Bay. Thick stands of trees lined riverbanks near the bay and game was plentiful. "All around is truly beautiful," he wrote to Palóu.

The Mission San Diego was the first permanent European settlement in Alta California.

California before Serra

Native Americans living in small, independent groups of hunter-gatherers flourished in California for thousands of years before the first European explorer ever visited the region. Among the hundreds of tribes living in California when Serra arrived were the Hupas and Pomos in the north, the Miwoks and Yokuts in central California, and the Chumashes in the south.

It is believed that Juan Rodríguez Cabrillo, a Portuguese explorer sailing under the flag of Spain, was the first European to see California. Traveling north from what is now Mexico, Cabrillo dropped anchor in San Diego Bay in September 1542 before continuing up the coast. The next major voyage along the coast was made in 1579 by the famous English sea captain Sir Francis Drake. He landed in northern California, probably across the bay from the present-day city of San Francisco, and claimed the region, which he called New Albion, for England.

Afraid that the English would establish settlements, the Spanish sent several expeditions to California, including one led by the explorer Sebastian Vizcaíno in 1602-1603. But no European settlements were established in the seventeenth century.

In the mid-1700s, there were rumors that Russians were establishing fur-trading settlements in California. The Spanish decided the time was right to stake their claim to the territory.

Serra failed to convert a single Indian in the mission's first year. But the Spaniards were not limiting themselves to this mission. Before the San Diego mission was even dedicated, Portolá took a group of soldiers and two priests north to find Monterey Bay, which had been described by explorer Sebastian Vizcaíno about 170 years earlier. Gálvez wanted to establish a settlement there to keep Russian trappers from entering Spanish territory.

Portolá failed to locate Monterey, so the expedition returned to San Diego six months later. They found the mission there in dire straits. An Indian attack had killed one of the party, and Serra and the others left at the mission were near starvation. The *San Antonio*, which had been sent back to Baja California for supplies, was feared lost at sea.

Portolá decided to wait until March 19 for the *San Antonio* to return with food. If the ship didn't arrive by then, he said, the mission would be abandoned. On March 11, Serra began a novena—nine days of prayer for a special purpose. On March 19, a ship's sails were spotted on the horizon. It was the *San Antonio*, arriving the last day of the novena.

Soon, Portolá set out for Monterey again. He went by land, while Serra made the voyage aboard the *San Antonio*. This time, the bay was easily found. In fact, Portolá had been there on his earlier journey north without recognizing it. On June 3, 1770, the mission was dedicated with a mass. Mission San Carlos, as this mission was called, became Father Serra's headquarters. A chapel and fort were soon built at the site of the present-day town of Carmel.

"All the heathen men go naked, with no other clothing than that which nature gave them. The women go modestly covered in front with strings which they wear tied at the waist. . . . Both men and women are much painted, and the men have the lobes of their ears pierced, from which they wear sea-shells."
—Father Juan Crespí, describing the Indians of southern California

"After preparing the altar, and hanging the bells from the branches of the tree, we sang the hymn *Veni, Creator* and blessed the holy water. We then raised aloft and blessed a great cross, likewise the royal standards. After that I celebrated the first Mass."
—Serra, describing the founding of the San Carlos mission

This painting of the San Carlos mission, made in 1791, shows the main mission grounds and the huts of the Indian workers. With its beautiful hilltop location, this mission was Serra's favorite.

In the years that followed, one mission after another was established. Serra founded Mission San Antonio south of Monterey on July 14, 1771; two months later, another Franciscan founded Mission San Gabriel near present-day Los Angeles. On September 1, 1772, Serra founded Mission San Luis Obispo, about halfway between San Francisco and Los Angeles.

As the Americans and the British fought the Revolutionary War on the other side of the continent, Father Palóu, under instructions from Serra, founded Mission San Francisco de Asis in what is now San Francisco in October 1776. The next month, Serra founded Mission San Juan Capistrano, the mission to which the swallows come each year on the feast of St. Joseph. Under Serra's guidance, Mission Santa Clara was dedicated on the site of today's city of Santa Clara, California, in January 1777. Then, on Easter Sunday, March 31, 1782, Father Serra founded his ninth and last mission, San Buenaventura, in what is now Ventura, California.

In those years, Serra worked ceaselessly, building missions and converting Indians. He also helped the Indians establish themselves as farmers and ranchers. By the end of that decade and a half, some 6,000 Indians had been converted and about 5,000 of those were living in villages close to the missions. Mission farms supported almost 15,000 head of cattle, sheep, horses, and other livestock. Mission fields

A map of the young United States in 1778

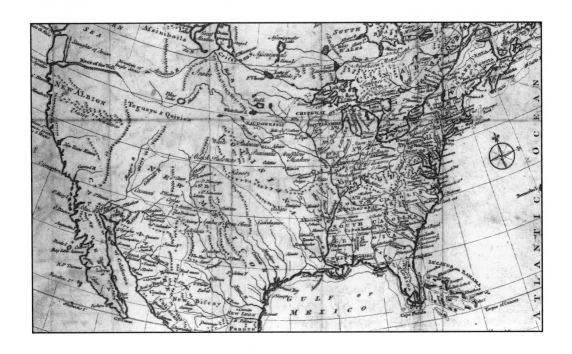

yielded about 17,000 bushels of wheat, barley, and other crops each year.

Serra also strove to protect the Indians from the Spanish military rulers. He drew up a legal document that placed the Indians in the care of the priests. Once, when a military commander arrested an Indian under the protection of the church, Serra called for the commander's excommunication (expulsion from the Catholic Church).

For two years following the founding of San Buenaventura, Serra visited each of his missions in turn. By that time, he was in his sixties and in constant pain. On August 28, 1784, after spending an entire night in prayer, he lay on a bed of plain wooden planks in his tiny room and clasped his crucifix to his chest. Then, in the words of Father Palóu, Junípero Serra "went to receive in heaven the rewards of his apostolic labors."

In 1934 Junípero Serra was nominated as a candidate for canonization, the process through which the Roman Catholic Church elevates people to sainthood. More than 50 years later, in 1986, the Roman Catholic Church announced that it was going to beatify Father Serra (the last step before sainthood). This news brought a storm of

This statue of Junípero Serra towers larger than life next to the San Francisco Bay Area's Junípero Serra Freeway, often called the most beautiful highway in the nation.

protest from American Indian groups who argued that the Spanish missionaries had tried to destroy Indian cultures. In response, Pope John Paul II admitted that excesses had been committed during those years, but he insisted that Serra was not guilty of wrongdoing. Instead, Serra had often protected the Indians. Serra was beatified on September 25, 1988, and became the Blessed Junípero Serra. It is not known if or when he will be declared a saint.

The Spanish Frontier in Transition

In the years following the establishment of the Catholic missions by Junípero Serra, only a few colonists from Mexico could be persuaded to move to the settlements. The Indians of California, while receiving some protection from the missionaries, were exploited and abused by their Spanish over-lords. Except for some of the interior tribes, California's Indian population declined steeply as Indians died from new diseases and harsh treatment.

Starting in September 1810, Mexico was torn by political upheavals that continued until 1821, when the nation gained independence from Spain. For a time, the Mexican government attempted to retain control of its provinces in Alta California and the rest of the Southwest, even as the opening of the Santa Fe Trail and other trails brought more Americans into the region. The effort to rule the faraway frontier territory, however, proved too costly and difficult. After the mid-1830s, Mexican colonists in California and the Southwest were largely abandoned by Mexico. While Mexico refused to officially relinquish control of the area, soldiers were withdrawn and *presidios*, or forts, were allowed to fall into disrepair. Some missions were closed, and many resident Indians were allowed to leave.

As the American population in California and the rest of the Southwest grew, Americans began to clamor for the United States to take control of the territory. As a result of the Mexican War, California became part of United States territory in 1848.

Chapter Four

John Sutter
and the
Opening of California

*I*n mid-August 1839, colonists traveling in three small boats landed where the Sacramento and American Rivers meet in central California. The motley group included 9 American-born fortune hunters, 10 Kanaka natives from the Hawaiian Islands, and a fierce bulldog. They were led by a 36-year-old former shopkeeper from Switzerland named Captain John Sutter. Over the next several years, Sutter, a genius at self-promotion, would establish a huge personal empire on the California frontier. Then came the gold rush.

Johann August Sutter (known to history as Captain John Sutter) was born shortly before dawn on February 15, 1803, in the village of Kandern in present-day Germany. His father, Johann Jakob Sutter, was a manager at a paper mill; his mother,

Captain John Sutter (1803-1880), in full military regalia, welcomes visitors to his California empire, New Helvetia.

61

Napoleon Bonaparte (1769-1821) rose out of the chaos of the French Revolution. By 1812, he had control of much of Europe, including Sutter's home region.

Christine, was the daughter of a minister. He had one brother, Jakob, born in 1808.

Kandern, in the years of Johann's early life, was a staging area for Prussian and Austrian troops on their way to battle Napoleon Bonaparte, the emperor of France. As he watched the military activity, Sutter began to fantasize about being a soldier. Indeed, he later claimed that he studied at a military academy as a boy and went on to become an officer in the Swiss army. Those claims were pure fiction. The truth was that in 1820, when Johann was about 17, he became an apprentice in a Basel, Switzerland, paper mill.

But young Johann Sutter proved to be unsuited for work in a paper mill. When his apprenticeship ended in 1823, he left the mill and struck out on his own. By 1824, Sutter was working as a clerk in a textile shop in the Swiss town of Aarburg.

In Aarburg, he met Annette Dübeld, the young woman who would become his wife. He fell head-over-heels in love with her. When Annette left Aarburg not long after they met, Sutter followed her to her hometown of Burgdorf, a beautiful medieval city. Even though he still dreamed of a life as a soldier and hero, he took a job as a clerk in a grocery store. He and Annette were married about two years later, on October 24, 1826. Custom dictated that they had to marry at this point, for on the very next day, Mrs. Sutter gave birth to a son. The boy was named Johann August, after his father.

As Sutter's family grew to include five children, he failed at one business venture after another and ran up huge debts. Finally, in May 1834, hounded by creditors, Sutter boarded a ship for America, leaving his wife and children behind. Annette helped him escape, thinking he would soon send for the family.

Sutter must have breathed a huge sigh of relief as soon as he was safely away from his creditors. He may also have been pleased to be free of his family, for he resented the financial burden. Annette had also been unhappy. John had never been able to provide financial stability, but perhaps things would now get better. John did not write for them to come, however, and Annette became dependent on the charity of her relatives.

Immediately after Sutter arrived in New York City in July 1834, he headed west to Missouri, then the westernmost state of the United States and the jumping-off place for settlers heading into the frontier. It was a perfect spot for a young man to find opportunity and, perhaps, earn a fortune.

For the next three years, as he slowly learned English, Sutter started a business as a trader, presenting himself as Captain John A. Sutter, a dashing military man. He made at least two trips overland from St. Louis to Santa Fe, New Mexico, selling shoes, fabric, farm implements, and other goods to settlers. For a time, he worked as a shopkeeper in the town of Westport, near Kansas City, Missouri. The success he sought, however, continued to elude him. By mid-1837, Sutter was bankrupt.

Sutter decided to see if his luck would be better in what was then Mexican California. He departed

"The hills and valleys are all covered with tall trees, but in such a manner that you might think an artist had here been at work creating a park," wrote Gottfried Duden about Missouri in a Swiss book Sutter may have read. "Here, if anywhere, it is possible to combine pleasure with utility."

from Missouri in the spring of 1838. The only safe way to travel across the western frontier in those days was in the company of other travelers, so Sutter went with a group of fur traders as far as the Rocky Mountains. There he joined a missionary caravan traveling to the northwestern frontier. He arrived in Fort Vancouver on the Columbia River, on the southern border of what is now the state of Washington, in October 1838.

While Sutter was anxious to reach California, it was too late in the season for an overland trek down the rugged west coast. Instead, he took a ship to Hawaii, then known as the Sandwich Islands, hoping to find passage from Honolulu to San Francisco (then called Yerba Buena). For five months, Sutter was stranded in Hawaii because no vessels were bound for the mainland. Finally, in late April 1839, he secured passage to California by way of Russian Alaska, and he arrived in Yerba Buena on July 1, 1839. His journey had taken more than a year.

California (then known by its Spanish name of Alta, or upper, California) was a province of Mexico. As a foreigner, Sutter had to present himself to the Mexican governor, Juan Bautista Alvarado, for permission to stay in California. So he headed to the capital of Monterey. By this time, the former shopkeeper and failed trader had added to his fictional military career, claiming he was a former officer in the Royal Swiss Guard of France. Sutter had picked up some Spanish in Santa Fe. This, along with his title and many letters of introduction written by important people he had met on his travels, endeared him to Alvarado. The Mexican governor gave him permission to settle a tract of land on the frontier to the north. After a year, Alvarado promised, this land would be permanently granted to Sutter.

After a brief stopover in Yerba Buena, Sutter went north to Sonoma to call on General Mariano Vallejo, Alvarado's uncle and the commander of the Mexican army in the region. Vallejo advised Sutter to find land close to San Francisco Bay, but the captain said he preferred to be on a navigable river. In reality, Sutter wanted to put some distance between himself and the Mexicans in California so that he could be his own boss. "I noticed," he remarked, "that the hat must come off before the military guard, the flagstaff, and the church, and I preferred a country where I could keep mine on."

Returning to Yerba Buena, Sutter chartered two supply vessels and bought another small boat to carry a party of colonists to his new outpost on the Sacramento River. His act as a captain and his letters of introduction were so convincing that he was able to obtain not only the vessels but also weapons, food, and farm implements on just a promise to pay in beaver pelts.

Sutter and his small party of colonists reached Carquinez Strait by what is now the city of Vallejo on August 8, 1839. Then they unloaded smaller boats and began their journey to Suisun Bay and the mouth of the Sacramento River. On August 13, after five days of difficult travel through hostile Indian territory, Sutter's party landed on the south bank of the Sacramento River where it joins the American

Mariano Vallejo (1808-1890), for whom the city of Vallejo, California, was named, maintained tight control over his territory, and he wanted to keep an eye on Sutter as well.

The area around the Sacramento River was described by an early explorer as being "like a park, because of the verdure [greenness] and luxuriance of its groves of trees."

River. The spot where Sutter landed was near the base of today's 28th Street in the city of Sacramento.

The site was as forbidding as it was lovely. Mosquitoes swarmed and the woods were alive with bears, wolves, and coyotes. Sutter was aware of the difficulties that lay ahead. The morning after their arrival, he offered transportation back to Yerba Buena to any who wished to return. Six whites departed. Sutter was left with 3 white settlers, the 10 Kanakas, an Indian boy, and his bulldog.

The Ochecame Indians of the region were already familiar with Europeans since they had been in contact with Spanish missionaries at the Mission San Jose (in what is now the city of Fremont). Sutter quickly established more-or-less friendly relations with the native inhabitants of the region by using a "carrot-and-stick" approach. On the one hand, he gave them gifts of beads, clothing, and blankets. On the other, he demonstrated his military might by firing one of several cannons he had brought from Honolulu. The Indians, he reported, "didn't care to have [the cannons] tried on them."

Following a quick exploration of the area, Sutter decided to establish his permanent camp on a rise about a mile south of the landing site. Forcing local Indians to work for him, he began building New Helvetia (New Switzerland). At first, Sutter lived in a tent while the other settlers lived in huts erected by the Kanakas. Using woven tule, a reed that grew in great abundance on the riverbank, the Kanakas formed huts like those of their native land. Soon an adobe structure about 45 feet long was built.

Helvetia was an ancient name for Switzerland, given to it by the Romans in the time of Julius Caesar.

This building housed Sutter's room, a blacksmith shop, and a kitchen for the settlement. A road was cut through the woods from the structure to the landing place at the river. Indian workers toiled for long hours in the fields around the settlement and did virtually all the manual labor involved in the building.

In August 1840, at the end of his required year of occupation, Sutter made the journey to Monterey. He received Mexican citizenship and became, as far as Mexico was concerned, Don Juan Augusto Sutter. As promised, Governor Alvarado granted him about 33 square miles of land around his settlement.

Alvarado had several motives in giving Sutter his grant. For one thing, the settlement provided a buffer between the Mexicans and the Indians. He also wanted an ally in his ongoing struggle for power with his uncle, General Vallejo. Finally, he hoped Sutter would protect Mexico's interests in California.

Captain John Sutter, the failed shopkeeper from Switzerland, had now realized his dream. He was an emperor in his own land and a military commander. Facing his first Indian attack just two months later, Sutter needed this power.

Sutter recruited more workers to build New Helvetia, paying them no more than food, shelter, and the promise of more substantial rewards in the future. Now that he owned the land, Sutter began to plant crops and raise cattle instead of just trapping beaver. He also began receiving important foreign guests—dignitaries, ambassadors, and spies. Despite his capacity as a Mexican official, Sutter saw himself

Sutter's land grant gave him the power "to represent in the Establishment of New Helvetia all the laws of [Mexico], to function as political authority and dispenser of justice, in order to prevent the robberies committed by adventurers from the Unites States, to stop the invasion of savage Indians and the hunting and trapping by companies from the [Northwest]."

as the holder of the key to California. Whichever nation wooed him best might win the reward.

A year after receiving his first land grant from Mexico, Sutter was awarded a second grant that substantially increased his holdings. Now he began to build his outpost into a town. At the center of the fortified settlement stood his new house, an adobe building with a main floor, attic, and basement. Around a large courtyard stood a wall reinforced with adobe bricks, 18 feet high and 3 feet thick. Eventually, a second, less formidable wall was built about 17 feet inside the outer wall. The space between these two walls was roofed over and divided into small rooms for workshops, storerooms, and living quarters.

Sutter's fort had "an imposing appearance at a distance," reported trapper James Clyman, "but on nearer inspection it is found that the whole Fort, houses and all, are built of . . . mud walls and covered inside and out with fleas, which grow here to the greatest perfection."

With as many as 1,000 potentially hostile Indians working for him at any time, Sutter had to manage supplies carefully and ensure adequate defenses. Sutter chose a select group of Indians and formed his own frontier army. Decked out in uniforms, these soldiers marched, practiced military exercises, and defended the fort—largely from other Indians. Sutter's success was due in large part to knowing just how much force to use to control the native population. During the next eight years, Sutter truly became an emperor in his own land.

With expansion on his mind, the captain purchased, on credit, two forts abandoned by Russian fur trappers. Sutter had no intention of using Fort Ross or Fort Bodega, located on the Pacific coast in what is now Marin County. Instead, he wanted the cattle, supplies, tools, and farm implements that were included in the sale.

Captain Sutter needed these items because his settlement sat right on an overland trail that led from the United States to California. Sutter's Fort, as it was soon known, became the destination of ever-increasing numbers of immigrants coming into California. Sutter was always ready to help these newcomers, providing shelter and food without charge. Many stayed on to settle near the fort on land Sutter allowed them to use. The captain regarded the immigrants as allies to strengthen his empire. One pioneer called him a "large-hearted, generous man" who supplied "everything [the] heart could wish." And, he added, "for all this the noble man declined any compensation."

U.S. Claims to California

Even after Meriwether Lewis and William Clark opened up the West to the United States with their expedition in 1804-1805, Americans were slow to invade the Mexican territory of California. In 1826, mountain man Jedediah Smith led a party overland, but other trappers did not follow him.

There was no reason at first for John Sutter to think that California would not remain Mexican. But, beginning in 1841, Americans began to arrive in wagon trains. The pioneers came to California overland at the same time that others were heading to the Northwest, Utah, and the Southwest. Like other settlers, they came to make a living by trapping furs or farming.

The arrival of the wagon trains coincided with the revolt of the Californios—Californians of Mexican descent—against rule by Mexico. The Californios kicked out their governor in 1845. In the midst of this unrest, Captain John C. Frémont led two surveying expeditions to California for the U.S. government in 1844 and 1846, stopping briefly at Sutter's Fort to obtain supplies. With Frémont's military help, U.S. settlers set up a makeshift republic in California in 1846.

The Americans in California raise the flag of the Bear Flag Republic on July 4, 1846, proclaiming their independence from Mexico on America's Independence Day.

Sutter's empire was like a house built on a foundation of sand. He was deeply in debt to the Russian government for the forts he had purchased. In addition, Sutter was forced, because of his position, to maintain friendly relations with the Mexican government even as he welcomed the streams of immigrants that flowed into California from the United States.

Friction between the United States and Mexico was growing in the 1840s as Mexico tried, unsuccessfully, to stem the flow of Americans into California and the rest of the Southwest. Tensions came to a head in May 1846 when the United States declared war on Mexico. The Mexican War lasted until early 1848. For a time, Sutter lost control of his fort when it was taken over by the U.S. Army under the command of Captain John C. Frémont. As part of the terms to end the war, California was ceded to the United States by Mexico. Sutter's Fort, which was restored to him, was now in U.S. territory.

By early 1847, when it was clear that the United States would win California, Sutter had expanded his holdings. He built a gristmill on the American River about 4 miles above his fort, planning to grind wheat for the entire Sacramento Valley. Since he needed lumber for his various projects, he also started construction of a sawmill about 40 miles east of the fort on a site outside his land grant.

This sawmill by what is now the town of Coloma would change American history and Sutter's life forever. In January 1848, sawmill manager James Marshall found pea-sized granules of ore he believed

A few days after Marshall told him about the gold, Sutter went to inspect the mill himself. He found gold in the American River and surrounding streams and swore all the workers to secrecy.

to be gold. He rushed to the fort and showed the ore to Sutter. Several experiments convinced Sutter that this was, indeed, "the finest kind of gold."

The captain feared the discovery of gold in his precious valley would turn his dream of empire into a nightmare. His concerns soon proved to be well founded. As news of the gold spread, Sutter's workers abandoned his mill, leather-tanning operation, blacksmith shop, and the other enterprises that supported Sutter's Fort.

Sutter tried to reap this unexpected harvest of wealth, but he was drinking heavily and was overwhelmed by the demands of trying to mine at Coloma and farm at New Helvetia. In his absence, people ransacked the fort. Thieves stole the barrels

Sutter used to cure salmon, took the bells from the fort's bell tower, and even heisted the millstone from his gristmill. The basement of his big adobe house became a saloon and gambling den.

Then help came from Sutter's oldest son, Johann (John) Jr., a stranger after 14 years of separation. John Jr.'s arrival in autumn 1848 relieved Sutter of some burdens. Dismayed by his father's alcoholism and the chaos at the fort, the 21-year-old tried (not very successfully) to straighten out Sutter's finances. But he managed to lay out Sacramento and eventually settled the debt to the Russians. To prepare for the family's reunion, John Jr. established a home away from the fort at Hock Farm, north of Sacramento on the Feather River.

As John Jr. muddled his way through complicated business affairs, Sutter threw himself into California politics. He was a delegate to the 1849 convention at which California's state constitution was drafted. He was also a losing candidate in the first election for governor of California. The next year, after 16 years of trying to raise the family by herself, Annette Sutter came to California with the other children. The family settled at Hock Farm.

Meanwhile, the Sacramento Valley became flooded with fortune hunters in what has since come to be known as the gold rush. The gold rush opened up the West as no missionary enterprise or fur-trapping operation ever could have. In 1849, 40,000 people arrived in San Francisco by boat and 6,000 wagons made their way across the continent. Americans were coming down with gold fever.

"Hardly a day passed . . . on which [Sutter] and his clerks, partners, Indians, etc., were not . . . intoxicated."
—John Sutter Jr.

California from the Gold Rush to Statehood

The flood of hopeful gold miners who arrived in California in 1849 were dubbed the 'Forty-Niners, but the numbers of immigrants kept rising dramatically for the next decade. There were 14,000 Californians in 1848. By 1860, there were 400,000.

In 1849, Californians began pushing for statehood to bring some sense of order to the violence and lawlessness of the gold rush. After debate in Congress over slavery, California entered the Union as a free state under the Compromise of 1850.

The increase in population and opportunities in California also encouraged the construction of wagon roads and, later, railroads. Work on the railroads brought many thousands of Chinese laborers into California. The huge task of the transcontinental railroad was not completed until 1869. As soon as an economic slump hit, the white settlers turned against the Chinese and called for their exclusion from the state. Whites burned down Chinese businesses and assaulted the men.

Still, many Chinese withstood the abuse and remained in California, and new Japanese immigrants established agricultural operations. Their success led to even more discrimination.

By the late 1800s, agriculture was California's major business. Since World War II, the defense industry has been a mainstay of the state's economy, only now rivaled by the computer industry.

Things went from bad to worse for Captain Sutter. After squatters moved onto his land, he spent much of the next decade in legal battles to prove his claim to property he had been given by the Mexican government. As a result of his drinking, mismanagement of his affairs, and falling victim to every con man who came around, Sutter's financial situation deteriorated to virtual pennilessness. When the U.S. Supreme Court handed down its decision in favor of the squatters, Sutter was left a broken man.

While Sutter was reduced to ruin, the region around his fort, fueled by the gold rush, blossomed into the bustling city of Sacramento. By the spring of 1850, Sacramento had a printing press, more than

Squatters are people who reside on land without having title to it. They are sometimes able to acquire legal rights to the land by living on it.

Sacramento in December 1849, just one year after it was planned by John Sutter Jr. John Jr.'s father was furious that the town was named Sacramento (for the river) instead of Sutter's City and was not located on the site he had chosen on higher ground.

two dozen stores, a pool hall, a bowling alley, and six bars that were also houses of prostitution.

There was no stopping the growth once it started. Although the Sacramento and American Rivers overflowed their banks in 1850 and flooded the town, Sacramento sprang up again as soon as the water receded. Then it was nearly destroyed by a fire. Floods struck again in 1852 and 1853. Miners in the throes of gold fever rebuilt it after each disaster, finally constructing a system of dams and dikes to protect the city from rising water. In 1854, the thriving community that stood by the site of Sutter's Fort became the capital of the state of California.

As Sacramento grew and prospered, Sutter's fortunes continued to slide. He and his son had strained relations over Sacramento and John Jr.'s failure to save his father from bankruptcy. John Jr. moved to Mexico and eventually became a successful businessman there. Sutter, in contrast, was forced to seek financial assistance from the California state legislature. In 1864, the state legislature granted him a pension of $250 per month, not enough to make much of a dent in his overwhelming debts.

Dissatisfied, Captain Sutter turned his pleas to the U.S. Congress the next year, moving east so he could be in Washington, D.C., when Congress was in session. For five years the family wintered in Washington and summered in Pennsylvania and elsewhere in the East. They finally settled permanently in Lititz, Pennsylvania, in 1870. While on yet another fruitless visit to Washington, John Sutter died suddenly in June 1880, at the age of 77.

"What a great misfortune was this sudden gold discovery for me! It has just broken up and ruined my hard, restless, and industrious labors. . . . By this sudden discovery of the gold, all my great plans were destroyed. . . . Instead of being rich, I am ruined."
—Sutter, in *Hutchings'
California Magazine*,
November 1857

Alaska and Hawaii to Statehood

Hawaii and Alaska, the far-flung colonial outposts John Sutter visited in 1838 and 1839, would be the last two states to join the Union—well over a century later.

Even though these states did not become part of the United States until 1959, their history of settlement is quite old. Alaska was the first region in North America that prehistoric hunters from Asia set foot in when they crossed the Bering Land Bridge (now the Bering Strait) more than 30,000 years ago.

It was over the Bering Strait that a more recent immigration to Alaska came as well. After several decades of trapping otters, Russian traders founded their first permanent settlement in Alaska on Kodiak Island in 1784. The Russian American Company, headquartered in Sitka, had a monopoly on the Alaskan fur trade by 1799.

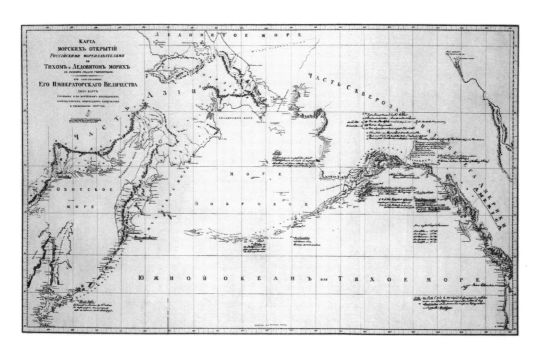

Russian Alaska in 1802. The Russian labels identify the Pacific Ocean (bottom), the Beaver Sea (Bering Sea) above that, and the territories of Asia (left) and the far west coast of America (right).

The Russian American Company gradually expanded south down the coast of North America, founding two forts in California in 1812 that would play a part in John Sutter's story. But confrontation with British and American fur-trading companies began to hem in the vast expanse of Russian Alaska. Its southern boundary was set at its current location in 1824. When Sutter visited in 1839, traders were still active, but Russian interest in Alaska was declining.

Distant Alaska became part of the United States in 1867, when Secretary of State William Seward insisted on its purchase, but it was called "Seward's Folly" by critics of the diplomat's decision. No governor was named until 1880, after gold was discovered. When the big gold strikes came in the late 1890s, thousands of miners came into Alaska. Miners brought gambling, drinking, and general lawlessness, prompting the territory to institute its first legal code in 1899. Still, it was not until 1906 that Alaska got its first territorial representative in the U.S. Congress and not until 1912 that it officially became a U.S. territory.

Over time, Alaska's economy became based on fishing. After World War II, when its strategic importance became clear, the territory experienced new growth, and its population doubled by 1960. Alaska became the 49th state on January 3, 1959.

Its main industries today are fishing, timber, and gas and petroleum drilling.

Unlike the rest of the United States, the first immigrants to the Hawaiian Islands were not the future American Indians, but Polynesians, who arrived about A.D. 750. Europeans first came in 1778, when Captain James Cook of England landed on the islands and named them the Sandwich Islands for the earl of Sandwich.

Americans began trading in Hawaii in the early nineteenth century, welcomed by King Kamehameha I. The traders brought more disease and alcohol than money for the Hawaiians, and the native population plummeted. When Sutter came in 1838, missionaries had arrived and founded schools and converted many Hawaiians.

Two years later, Hawaii established a constitutional monarchy, and from 1842 to 1854 American G. P. Judd was the prime minister. Sugar plantations worked by Asians sprung up, and Americans began investing in the industry later in the century. The United States had no claim to territory in Hawaii, but it had a good trading agreement and enough influence that the U.S. was given permission to establish a naval base at Pearl Harbor in 1887.

In 1893, the monarchy was overthrown and Hawaii became a U.S. protectorate with a provisional government of mostly American-born residents. To his credit,

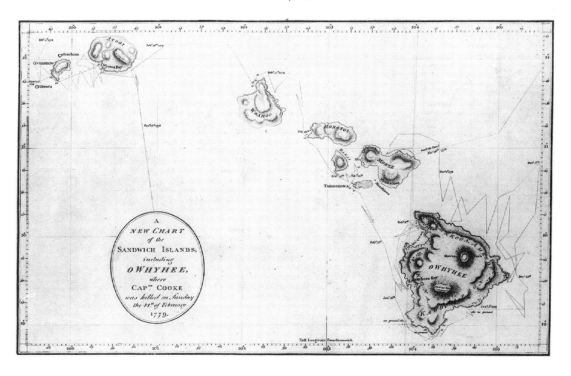

The eight Sandwich Islands (Hawaii), 1779. The natives at first thought Captain Cook was a god and showered him with gifts. When Cook returned in 1779, they were enraged when they realized he was not a god. He was killed in a gruesome attack.

President Grover Cleveland refused to annex Hawaii when he found out native Hawaiians did not support the overthrow of the monarchy or the rule of American Sanford Dole's provisional government. But President William McKinley, who succeeded Cleveland, sided with the Americans and annexed the islands for the United States in 1898. In 1900, Hawaii became a U.S. territory governed by Sanford Dole.

The December 7, 1941, attack on Pearl Harbor in World War II revealed Hawaii's military importance. This security need, coupled with the growth of American tourism after the war, gave Hawaii the statehood it had sought since 1937. It became the 50th state on August 21, 1959.

Chapter Five

John McLoughlin
and the
British Northwest

On a July day in 1824, two large canoes departed from the fur-trading center of York Factory on the Hudson Bay in northern Manitoba, Canada. John McLoughlin, a physician and fur trader, rode in one of the canoes. Dressed in the dark suit and tall beaver hat worn by gentleman fur traders, "Dr. John," as he was called, must have been a striking sight. He was six feet, four inches tall, and his thick mane of hair was pure white, even though he was not yet 40 years old.

For two decades Dr. John had been stationed at forts around northern Lake Superior. Now he was on his way to Fort George in Astoria, Oregon, at the mouth of the Columbia River. There he would oversee the business of the Hudson's Bay Company, the largest fur-trading company in North America.

With his shock of white hair, piercing eyes, and sharp features, John McLoughlin (1784-1857) was called the "White-Headed Eagle" by the Indians of the Columbia River region.

John McLoughlin (pronounced "McLawklin") was born in what is now the province of Quebec, Canada, on October 19, 1784, the third of John and Angélique McLoughlin's eight children. John's hometown was the village of Rivière du Loup, downstream from Quebec City on the St. Lawrence River. His father, a farmer, was from Ireland; his mother was of French and Scottish ancestry.

At the age of 14, John became an apprentice to a physician in Quebec so he could learn medicine. Soon after he finished the apprenticeship, "Dr. John" joined the North West Company as a physician for fur-trading posts.

According to a McLoughlin family tale, John joined the North West Company as a means of escape. He had gotten into a scuffle with a British army officer who was rude to a woman John was dating. The British ruled Canada, so John needed to get out of town.

From America's colonial period onward, high hats made of beaver fur had been fashionable in both America and Europe, driving a demand for beaver pelts. The English and French had fought wars for control of profitable beaver territories. As beavers were hunted to scarcity in settled areas, the search for pelts sent trappers into the remote Northwest. By the early 1800s, the Nor'West Company, as it was often called, was one of two British trading companies that dominated the North American fur trade. The other was the Hudson's Bay Company.

Early on, John McLoughlin called his decision to work for the company a "sad experiment" because he was so lonely.

In early 1804, Dr. John was sent by the Nor'West Company to be the resident physician at Fort William on the north shore of Lake Superior, near the present-day city of Thunder Bay, Ontario. He quickly displayed as much talent for trading as for medicine. Dr. John spent the next several summers trading at Fort William, and he wintered at smaller outposts in the region.

Although he had a son, Joseph, by a Chippewa woman, Dr. John was not married when he met Marguerite McKay sometime between 1809 and 1811. The widow of a former Nor'West Company trader, Marguerite was half Chippewa and almost a full decade older than McLoughlin. She had four children. A gentle and charming woman, her calm nature was the perfect counterpoint for Dr. John's excitable one. They were married in late 1811 or early 1812. In August 1812, their first child, a son named John Jr., was born. John and Marguerite had three more children: Eliza, Eloisa, and David.

Dr. John traveled from fort to fort around northern Lake Superior when the children were small, returning whenever possible to visit his family at Fort William. He became the fort's chief trader and one of the most powerful men in the company.

Meanwhile, competition between the Hudson's Bay Company and Nor'West and was pushing both companies to the brink of financial ruin. In late 1820 and early 1821, Dr. John took part in meetings held in London to discuss a resolution. Finally, the rivals hammered out an agreement to merge and retain the name of the Hudson's Bay Company.

Dr. John became a close friend and trusted associate of George Simpson, the new governor-in-chief, as the company's North American director was called. At the annual company meeting in York Factory in 1824, Simpson named Dr. John the new factor, or director, of Fort George, the Hudson's Bay Company fort that had taken over the old Pacific Fur Company settlement at Astoria, Oregon.

Sir George Simpson (1792?-1860) had been with the Hudson's Bay Company before the merger. He became governor-in-chief of the newly united company's operations in Canada and the Northwest in 1821.

The Northwest before McLoughlin

In the centuries before Europeans came, the Northwest was densely populated by American Indians. Abundant resources such as wood and salmon made these village-based cultures wealthy, and they developed wide trading networks. The Indians fashioned elaborate totem poles, masks, and other artwork, and they had complex religious systems. Rich village leaders held potlatches—huge and expensive feasts—to boast their wealth.

Most Indians living north of the Columbia River spoke a Nez Perce language. Those south of the Columbia spoke Chinook languages. They traveled by canoe, and they fished, hunted, and gathered wild food. The inland Nez Perce hunted buffalo on horseback after the Spaniards introduced wild horses to North America in the sixteenth century.

The coastal reaches of Washington and Oregon were explored as early as the sixteenth century by Spanish and English sailors hoping to find the Northwest Passage—a waterway through the North American continent. It was not until 1775, however, that a Spanish expedition actually came ashore. In 1778, Captain James Cook became the first Englishman to visit the area. American captain Robert Gray discovered the mouth of the Columbia River in 1792, establishing American claim to the

American Robert Gray (1755-1806) was trapping sea otters for their pelts when he sailed into the Columbia River (named for his ship) on May 11, 1792.

region. That same year, British sea captain George Vancouver explored the coastline and completed the area's first maps.

The fur trade in this period was limited to sea-otter pelts. Following the overland exploration of the region by Americans in the early 1800s, land-based fur trading began. By the second decade of the nineteenth century, the Nor'West Company and the Pacific Fur Company owned by John Jacob Astor were competing for pelts in the region. Astor's company had founded the trading center of Astoria, Oregon, in 1811, but the turmoil of the War of 1812 led to its seizure by the British, who renamed it Fort George.

In the 1820s, the territory west of the Rockies, all the way from the boundaries of California and New Mexico to Alaska, was claimed by both England, which hoped to expand its holdings in Canada, and the United States, which had visions of a nation stretching from sea to sea. Under an 1818 agreement, citizens of both countries could enter the territory for trading purposes, but traders knew that whoever established themselves more securely would likely win the land dispute.

As the new chief of the Hudson's Bay Company's Columbia district, Dr. John was supposed to keep Americans out of the region. He was also instructed to develop the fur trade, establish good relations with the Indians in the area, and make Fort George self-sufficient.

On July 27, 1824, Dr. John and his party—which included Marguerite, six-year-old Eloisa, and three-year-old David—departed from York Factory, where Dr. John had received his new assignment. Simpson, who wanted to inspect Fort George, followed about three weeks later. Their 1,600-mile canoe trek took them across the wilderness of western Canada. The travelers endured cold nights,

Fur-trading company canoes were paddled by hard-working "voyageurs," usually French Canadians making meager wages, while the highly paid company officials sat back and directed them.

thick fogs, storms, and swarms of mosquitoes. Often, canoes and supplies had to be carried from one river to another. At times, rivers were so low that the canoes had to be dragged through mud.

On the morning of September 26, the McLoughlin party was overtaken by the governor and his group. After a journey of over three months, the two groups reached the mouth of the Columbia River and Fort George on November 8.

Since Fort George had originally been owned by the American John Jacob Astor (who had called it Astoria), Americans might claim a right to use it at any time because of the joint-occupancy agreement. So Dr. John and Simpson began scouting for a location for a new fort. McLoughlin soon found one: a bluff on the north bank of the Columbia River near the mouth of the Willamette River.

On March 19, 1825, Simpson formally dedicated the newly built Fort Vancouver. Later that day, the governor departed, leaving Dr. John in charge of a territory much larger than Great Britain. Dr. John soon added buildings and cleared nearby land for planting. While no exact description exists of the first Fort Vancouver, it would have had a stout palisade of closely fitted beams. Inside the palisade stood several buildings, including a house for the McLoughlin family. In 1829, Dr. John decided to move the thriving fort closer to the Columbia River, where canoes and boats were loaded and unloaded; a new fort was completed the next year.

Dr. John's first order of business was to establish good relations with the Chinooks, Multnomahs,

John Jacob Astor (1763-1848), who immigrated to America with no money in 1784, died the nation's wealthiest man. He founded the American Fur Company in 1808, the parent of the Pacific Fur Company that was headquartered in Astoria, Oregon.

and other Indians in the area. Despite opportunities for trade, he also sought to make Fort Vancouver self-supporting. The long workday at the fort began at 5 A.M. with the ringing of a great bell in the court-yard. McLoughlin spent part of each day visiting the workers in the fort, asking questions and shouting in his booming voice when things were not going well. He also regularly visited the fur-trapping outposts under his control.

In 1828, Governor Simpson came for a long stay at the fort. Gentleman visitors like Simpson and resident officials enjoyed all the trappings of civilization at Fort Vancouver. Dr. John and George Simpson must have sat for hours deep in conversa-tion, drinking imported wine and eating at tables set with fine blue and white china and silver candelabra.

Governor Simpson and Dr. John explored the Willamette River and claimed lands for the Hudson's

According to a visitor in the early 1840s, Fort Vancouver had "35 wooden buildings, used as officers' dwelling, lodging apartments for clerks, storehouses for furs, goods and grains; and as workshops. . . . One building near the rear gate is occupied as a school house. . . . Below the fort, and on the bank of the river, is a village of 53 wooden houses. . . . In these live the company's servants."

George Simpson was confident that Fort Vancouver would flourish because "the climate [was] so fine that Indian corn and other grain cannot fail of thriving."

Bay Company about 40 miles south of Fort Vancouver at the falls of the Willamette. Simpson praised Dr. John as "a very bustling active man" and "a good hearted man and a pleasant companion." An omen of things to come, however, he also took note of McLoughlin's temper. "A difference of opinion," commented Governor Simpson, "almost amounts to a declaration of hostilities."

Far removed from the headquarters of the Hudson's Bay Company, McLoughlin often had to make decisions on his own. Sometimes these actions differed from the policies of the Hudson's Bay Company and the recommendations of Governor Simpson. For example, Dr. John was supposed to control all fur trading in the region, but if he used force against American traders, he risked war. McLoughlin's solution was ingenious. Whenever he learned an American trading vessel was in the area, he sent men to pay more for all fur pelts brought to the ship for sale and also authorized them to sell any needed supplies to trappers for less than the Americans were asking. The Americans were thus locked out of trade without any use of force.

In order to dominate trade in the region, in the 1830s Dr. John started forts up and down the Pacific coast, stretching all the way to Russian Alaska. This strategy directly conflicted with that of Governor Simpson, who believed that trading ships were both cheaper and more efficient than forts.

Although Fort Vancouver was flourishing, Dr. John faced problems. In 1834 and 1836, American missionaries came to the Oregon country to preach

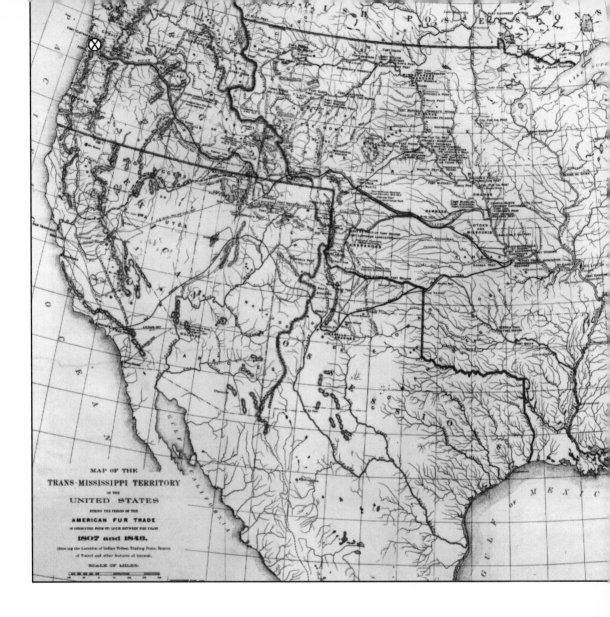

MAP OF THE
TRANS-MISSISSIPPI TERRITORY
OF THE
UNITED STATES
DURING THE PERIOD OF THE
AMERICAN FUR TRADE
AS CONDUCTED FROM ST. LOUIS BETWEEN THE YEARS
1807 and 1843.
Showing the Location of Indian Tribes, Trading Posts, Routes
of Travel and other features of interest.
SCALE OF MILES.

to the Indians. He had been instructed to protect the region from the Americans, but Dr. John, a devout Christian, donated land and money to help the missionaries in their work. The missionaries, in turn, sent back glowing descriptions of Oregon to their countrymen. These reports soon spurred a massive migration of Americans to the region.

Astor's American Fur Company dominated the American fur trade in McLoughlin's time. While the British controlled the Canadian trade, the Northwest, including Astoria (marked with an "x") was under contention.

U.S. Claims to the Northwest

By the late 1700s, Americans had made no attempt to settle the land between the Mississippi River and the Pacific Coast. But after Robert Gray discovered the Columbia River, American interest in finding a water route through the continent grew. Once the Louisiana Purchase of 1803 cemented U.S. claims to much of the nation's interior, President Thomas Jefferson decided the time was right to explore the continent.

Jefferson outfitted an expedition under the joint command of Meriwether Lewis and William Clark. The Corps of Discovery, as the party was called, left St. Louis, Missouri, on May 14, 1804, and reached the Pacific Ocean on November 15, 1805.

While Lewis and Clark failed to find a water route to the Pacific, they succeeded in a more important way. A route through the vast middle of North America had been explored and mapped for the first time.

Settlement was stalled by two main obstacles. The British also claimed the Northwest, but this issue was temporarily resolved in 1818 with the joint-occupancy agreement. More daunting was traveling Lewis and Clark's torturous route, but in 1824 trapper Jedediah Smith opened an easier path over the South Pass of the Rockies in Wyoming. Slowly traders, then missionaries, and finally pioneer families began moving west on what became known as the Oregon Trail.

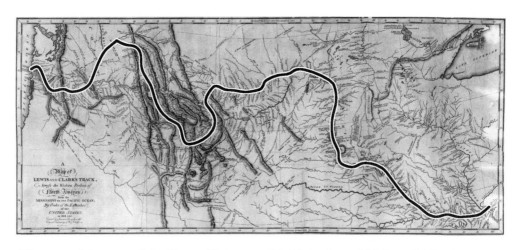

This map of the route of the Corps of Discovery (highlighted roughly) from St. Louis, Missouri, to the Pacific Ocean was based on William Clark's drawings.

Dr. John's independence would later come to haunt him. In 1841, the first signs of serious trouble between the governor and McLoughlin appeared. McLoughlin had named his son-in-law, William Glen Rae, chief of remote Fort Stikine on the coast of Alaska in 1840. McLoughlin's oldest son, John Jr., was assigned to aid William. But William resigned the position in Alaska in the spring of 1841. John Jr. was left alone, surrounded by hostile Indians and troublesome trappers and traders. In June, without consulting Dr. John, Simpson removed John Jr.'s only trusted assistant from the fort, leaving the unprotected young man with the rough traders.

Sir George (Simpson had been knighted for his service to the British) delivered this news to Dr. John in late October 1841, when he visited Fort Vancouver. He also ordered the closure of several of McLoughlin's northern forts and a fort in San Francisco that William Glen Rae had opened. The string of forts would be replaced by a trading ship. In a final insult, Dr. John was instructed to move his headquarters to a new fort on Vancouver Island in Puget Sound. Simpson was ruining all of Dr. John's work, and McLoughlin was furious! Both men scribbled out a series of angry letters for the company records while they argued face to face.

Dr. John's feelings turned to rage in June 1842 when he learned that John Jr. had been murdered. That tragic news came in an unsympathetic, almost brutal letter written by Sir George. In his letter, Simpson called young John's conduct at the fort "exceedingly bad." The murder, stated Simpson, was an act of self-defense because of John Jr.'s cruelty and drunken behavior.

For the next year, the grieving Dr. John fought to defend his son's honor. He discovered that the men at Fort Stikine were angry because John Jr. punished them for stealing supplies and sneaking Indian women into the fort at night. One trapper described young John's killing as deliberate murder. Still, Dr. John could not convince Simpson to charge the killers or clear his son's name.

During the next several years, Dr. John's troubles grew as the number of Americans moving into the region soared. As he had helped the missionaries, McLoughlin also extended aid to the pioneers.

Emigrants crossing the plains on the Oregon Trail and other trails west came in covered wagons pulled by teams of oxen. These wagons were soon dubbed "prairie schooners" after schooners, a kind of ship, because they appeared to be sailing on a sea of green in the tall-grass prairies.

He rescued stranded and starving parties and provided food and seed for crops on credit.

Once the Americans became established, however, the United States wanted full control of the region. The battle cry, "Fifty-Four Forty or Fight!" was heard across the country. Americans now wanted all the territory up to the southern border of Russian-held Alaska (latitude 54 degrees, 40 minutes north, which is Alaska's border with Canada today). War loomed between England and America.

McLoughlin was involved in his own legal battle over land at the falls of the Willamette River. In 1842, in an effort to stave off claims by Americans and some of the very missionaries he had helped, he had built a sawmill and hired a surveyor to lay out a town he called Oregon City. That plan, which was intended to establish proof of ownership, failed, and Dr. John was forced to buy his own land—*twice*—at a cost of about $6,500, a small fortune in 1844.

Still, Dr. John's trials were not over. In June 1845, word came that William Glen Rae, Eloisa's husband, had taken his own life at the fort in San Francisco. Not long after that, the Hudson's Bay Company's directors censured, or severely criticized, Dr. John for aiding American settlers.

As punishment, McLoughlin was removed as superintendent of the Columbia region and replaced by a committee of three men. And Dr. John was told he would be sent to a different post, far away from the region he'd called home for more than 20 years. Under the law, he could only hold his claim on the Willamette if he was a resident. That meant he must

"I cannot speak too highly of [McLoughlin], for his kindness to us all. He sent several boats loaded with provisions to meet the emigrants last fall, and continued to distribute little luxuries amongst us as we remained in reach of him—he is always on the lookout for an opportunity to bestow his charity, and bestows with no sparing hand."
—a pioneer's report, December 4, 1844

An official Hudson's Bay Company report charged that without McLoughlin's help, "not thirty American families would now have been in the settlement. . . . Had it not been for the trading posts of the Hudson's Bay Company they must have been starved or cut off by the Indians."

either forfeit his land or resign. In 1846, Dr. John reluctantly chose resignation.

John McLoughlin could not believe what had happened. He had worked hard for the company and built permanent settlements at Fort Vancouver and Oregon City. He had dealt fairly with the Indians and with his trappers. In an extremely difficult situation, he had avoided violent conflict with the Americans. And now, with his son and son-in-law dead, he had been forced to resign. "I have drunk and am drinking the cup of bitterness to the very dregs," he wrote.

In January 1846, Dr. John had moved to Oregon City after building a new home there. Marguerite joined him there, along with the widowed Eloisa and her children. Oregon City had already become a flourishing little town, with a population of 500. There were 80 houses, 2 churches, 2 bars, a number of shops, and the offices of the first newspaper on the Pacific Coast, the *Spectator*.

After so many years as ruler of Fort Vancouver, Dr. John found it difficult to be an ordinary citizen. He opened a flour mill and rented out his sawmill. Over time, he began to enjoy his new life. Eloisa's three children filled his house with laughter. The family was close, and Eloisa stayed there even after she remarried.

The dispute over who owned Oregon and Washington was settled in 1846, the year that brought so many other changes in McLoughlin's life. Surrounded by Americans, most of whom were grateful for all his generosity, Dr. John welcomed

the change. He applied to become a citizen of his adopted land in 1849 and looked forward to a life of peace and security as an American.

Once again, however, greed prevailed over justice. In 1850, a group of wealthy men who wanted McLoughlin's valuable Oregon City land convinced Congress not to honor his land claim—despite the fact that he had paid for it twice! The only saving grace was that the local government, which could not be deceived as easily as congressmen in faraway Washington, D.C., allowed him to live in his house and keep his businesses.

John McLoughlin's house in Oregon City is now a museum honoring the British fur trader as the father of Oregon.

This statue of John McLoughlin stands on the grounds of the State Capitol in Salem, Oregon.

For the rest of his life, Dr. John fought Congress over the rights to his land. Often, he was seen walking the streets of Oregon City, angrily waving his cane, denouncing the new government and the ingratitude of many of the people he had helped. The constant worry about his land took its toll, and by the summer of 1857 John McLoughlin was bedridden. He died on September 3, 1857, surrounded by his family.

On October 17, 1862, the Oregon State Legislature allowed Eloisa and her husband to purchase the family property for a token payment of $1,000.

Oregon from Territory to Statehood

Wagon trains rolled into Oregon for a year before a territorial government was established in 1843. To encourage immigration to the territory (and help secure the U.S. claim), married men were awarded 640 acres of land for settlement.

As Americans flowed into the region, the United States and England heatedly debated the Oregon Question, the dispute over ownership of territory all the way up to 54 degrees, 40 minutes latitude. In 1846, the "Question" was answered, and the northern boundary of U.S. territory was established at 49 degrees latitude, which remains the U.S.-Canadian border.

Still, the territory was not officially organized until the massacres of Marcus and Narcissa Whitman by Indians in 1847 spurred the U.S. government to action.

The Oregon Territory, which included what is now Washington as well as Idaho and parts of Montana and Wyoming, was created in 1848. The Washington Territory split off five years later.

Thousands of new settlers now moved to the land. They were attracted first by a short-lived gold rush. Providing supplies for California's gold rush proved a more lasting boon to the young region's economy. Soon its future looked promising, and Oregon was admitted to the Union as the 33rd state on February 14, 1859.

Wheat farming and cattle and sheep ranching became—and remain—important to the state's growth. And once railroad lines were completed across the country in the 1880s, Oregon's seemingly endless forests fueled its huge timber industry.

Chapter Six

The Whitmans
and the
Mission in Washington

On a February evening in 1836, a wedding was held in the Presbyterian church in the little town of Angelica, New York. The groom was 33-year-old Marcus Whitman. Narcissa Prentiss, a month shy of 28, was the bride.

After the couple exchanged vows, the preacher delivered a sermon. Then, as the ceremony drew to a close, the church congregation broke into song, with Narcissa's lovely voice carrying over the rest:

"Yes, my native land! I love thee;
All thy scenes I love thee well;
Friends, connections, happy country,
Can I bid you all farewell?
Can I leave thee, can I leave thee,
Far in heathen lands to dwell?"

Dr. John McLoughlin (with hand extended) welcomes Narcissa Whitman (reaching for McLoughlin's hand), Marcus Whitman (in top hat), and other pioneers to the Oregon country's Fort Vancouver on the Columbia River.

No hymn was more fitting for the marriage of Marcus and Narcissa Whitman. Soon after their wedding, they headed west as missionaries to the region we know today as the state of Washington.

Born on September 4, 1802, in a log cabin near Rushville, New York, Marcus was the third son of Beza and Alice Whitman. Marcus's early life was probably filled with hard work helping his family. His father had a shoemaking and leather-tanning shop, and his mother had constant duties on what was then the New York frontier. When Marcus was seven, his father died, and the family was torn apart.

Marcus was sent to live with an uncle near Plainfield, Massachusetts. His uncle was a devout Christian, and young Marcus began to experience the religious leanings that would color the rest of his life. At the age of about 16, he had what was called a "conversion" and formally dedicated his life to God.

Marcus returned to Rushville when he was 18. He became active in his church there, teaching Sunday school and leading sunrise prayer services. Marcus desperately wanted to become a minister, but he could not afford the necessary schooling.

For a time, Marcus worked in his father's old tannery and shoemaking shop. At the age of 21, he decided to become a physician. He apprenticed with a local doctor for the next two years, learning the basics of medicine. Following this on-the-job training, he enrolled in the College of Physicians and Surgeons in Fairfield, New York. After completing a program at the college that lasted just 16 weeks, Marcus Whitman was licensed to practice medicine.

In the late 1700s and early 1800s, America was swept by religious revivals that earned the name the Second Great Awakening. (The first one had occurred a half century earlier.) The Second Great Awakening led to a great interest in missionary work, both on the American frontier and throughout the world.

He later returned for a second 16-week term and earned a doctor of medicine degree.

For the next nine years, Marcus worked as a doctor in Canada and several New York towns. Yet the physician still dreamed of becoming a missionary. In the summer of 1834, he applied to the American Board of Commissioners for Foreign Missions, the Protestant organization in charge of missions. He was rejected because of health problems.

Several months after his rejection, Whitman heard a minister named Samuel Parker speak about the need for missionaries to serve the American Indians in the West. Whitman applied again to the American Board. In January, the board accepted his application. Whitman was assigned to accompany Parker on a journey to determine where a mission might be started west of the Rocky Mountains.

For the next few weeks, Marcus prepared to begin his work as a missionary doctor. After packing and visiting his family in Rushville, he went to Amity (now Belmont), New York. He may have gone there partly to meet with a young woman named Narcissa Prentiss. He knew the Prentiss family because he had practiced medicine near a town where they had lived. Now Narcissa also hoped to be a missionary. Marcus and Narcissa spent many hours together that February weekend, probably discussing religion and their hope of converting Indians. By the end of the weekend, they were engaged to be married. They would do their missionary work together.

Born on March 14, 1808, in the small town of Prattsburg, New York, Narcissa was the third of nine

Samuel Parker (1779-1866), a Congregational and Presbyterian minister, discovered his life's passion when he learned that a group of Indians west of the Rocky Mountains had come all the way to St. Louis in search of Christianity.

Narcissa's birthplace in Prattsburg. The Prentisses were one of the first families in the frontier village when they moved there in 1805.

children. Stephen and Clarissa Prentiss, Narcissa's parents, were both active churchgoers and, in time, so was their eldest daughter. After formally joining the church at age 11, Narcissa inspired the congregation singing hymns in her beautiful voice.

When Narcissa was growing up, there was no school for girls in Prattsburg, so she was probably educated at home by her parents. In 1827, when she was 19, the Franklin Academy in Prattsburg began accepting female students. Narcissa studied there the next year and took some more courses a few years later. It is thought she also attended college in Troy, New York. For a while, the young woman was a schoolteacher.

In June 1834, the Prentiss family, including 26-year-old Narcissa, moved about 40 miles southwest of Prattsburg to the town of Amity. Five months later, Rev. Samuel Parker came to Amity to recruit missionaries. Narcissa was captivated by a sermon much like the one Marcus Whitman had heard a few days earlier. After the meeting, Narcissa approached Parker. "Is there a place," she asked, "for an unmarried female in my Lord's vineyard?"

Parker wrote to the American Board inquiring if it would grant commissions to young women missionaries. But the board was unwilling to send single women into the wilderness. "I don't think we have missions among the Indians where unmarried females are valuable just now," the board wrote to Parker in late December 1834. After all, no white woman had ever crossed the Rocky Mountains.

The only way Narcissa could travel west as a missionary was as a married woman with her husband. In late February 1835, Marcus Whitman came to visit on his way to meet Parker in St. Louis. Their marriage plans gave Narcissa a second chance. She reapplied to the American Board, and in mid-March that appointment was approved.

While Narcissa was waiting to hear from the American Board, Marcus traveled to St. Louis, then the jumping-off point for almost all travelers headed to the West. There, he and Parker made arrangements to travel west with a caravan of fur traders from the American Fur Company. Whitman and Parker would journey with the caravan as far as the Green River in what is now western Wyoming.

By the time Narcissa was 16 years of age, she knew she wanted to be a missionary. "I frequently desired to go to the heathen but only half-heartedly," she wrote 10 years later, "and it was not till the first Monday of Jan. 1824 that I felt to consecrate [devote] myself without reserve to the missionary work waiting the leadings of Providence concerning me."

"These [mountain men] with their obstreperous mirth; their whooping, and howling, and quarreling, added to the mounted Indians who are constantly dashing into and through our camp, yelling like fiends; the barking and baying of savage wolf-dogs, and the incessant crackling of rifles and carbines render our camp a perfect bedlam."
—John Townsend, an observer of the 1834 Green River Rendezvous

After a rough journey, the caravan finally reached the Green River, the site of a fur-trading rendezvous, on August 12. The rendezvous was an annual event. Trappers from the West made their way to a predetermined spot in July and August, where they would meet with wagon trains from the East and trade pelts for supplies. Soon the gatherings, including the Green River Rendezvous, grew into carnival-like festivals lasting several weeks. Hundreds of trappers and thousands of Indians spent the time drinking, playing cards, and swapping stories. While Parker and Whitman were at Green River, they met some of the mountain men, including Jim Bridger, who had opened much of the West to American settlement.

The Mountain Men and Western Settlement

The mountain men who roamed the West in search of furs during the first half of the nineteenth century were the advance guard of the American westward expansion that was to come. In their time, these trappers and hunters were heroes idolized as much as movie stars and great athletes are today. Newspapers were filled with their exploits, both real and imagined. None were more famous than Jim Bridger and Jedediah Smith, two men who were largely responsible for opening up the settlement of vast areas of the West.

In 1824, Jedediah Smith learned an easier way across the Rockies from a party of Crow Indians. This mountain pass in Wyoming became known as South Pass to distinguish it from the northern pass crossed by Meriwether Lewis and William Clark 20 years earlier. Because the South Pass had a gentle ascent and descent, wagons and settlers could cross it to get to the Oregon Territory, Utah, or California.

In the years following that discovery, Smith led a party pioneering a route to California through the desert Southwest and the Sierra Nevada, as well as an overland trail from California north to the Columbia River. From the Columbia, he traveled across the mountains to Pierre's Hole in Idaho. Smith's treks opened many of the West's important trails, including the Oregon Trail and the Mormon Trail.

When they met at the 1835 rendezvous, Marcus Whitman operated on Jim Bridger to remove an arrowhead lodged in his back. Whitman was surprised that the wound wasn't infected, but Bridger responded, "Meat jes don't spoil in the mountains." In 1838, Bridger and another trapper began making plans to found a fort and trading post west of the South Pass, not far from the site of the Green River Rendezvous. Over the next five years, he built Fort Bridger in southwest Wyoming. Fort Bridger became an important station on the Oregon Trail and was also a military post and pony express station.

By the mid-1840s, the fur trade was beginning to die out. Beaver hats, long a requirement for any fashionable gentleman, went out of style. With the decline of the beaver trade, the romantic days of the mountain men were over.

Fort Bridger, Wyoming, in 1849. The site is now a state park, and some of the original buildings are still standing.

At the Green River Rendezvous, the missionaries had discussions with leaders of the Flathead and Nez Perce Indians. Christianity, the tribes believed, would give them special powers, and they asked the men to establish missions in their territory. Parker, with a guide, continued on to the Northwest. Whitman returned east to Narcissa.

Having seen wagons successfully negotiating the torturous Oregon Trail, Whitman was convinced that women could make the journey over the mountains. He brought this news to Narcissa in early December 1835, when he visited her in her family's new home in Angelica, a village six miles north of Amity. As they made their wedding plans, another missionary couple—Henry Spalding and his wife, Eliza—were approved by the missionary board to go west with Marcus and Narcissa.

Henry Spalding (1803-1874) poses with a Bible and a hoe, the twin tools of his missionary work among the Indians in the Oregon country.

Spalding was no stranger to Narcissa. In fact, years earlier Spalding had courted her and asked her to marry him. Narcissa had turned him down. The Whitmans believed this was all in the past, however. Since the American Board was having trouble finding missionaries, Marcus and Narcissa suggested the Spaldings.

In early March, only a couple weeks after exchanging their wedding vows, the Whitmans traveled by steamer to Liberty, Missouri. In Liberty, the two couples met an assistant, William H. Gray, who had been appointed by the American Board to accompany them, and hired two other men. They bought supplies for the overland part of the journey and livestock for their missions.

Almost 2,000 miles of prairie and several mountain ranges stretched ahead. The missionary party ran into difficulties right away. Plans to travel with an American Fur Company caravan went awry when the caravan departed without them on May 1. It was not safe to travel by themselves, so Whitman and the others pursued the caravan across more than 300 miles of rough terrain, fording rivers as best they could and driving the livestock. Finally, the exhausted party overtook the caravan on May 26, near the Platte River in eastern Nebraska.

On July 4, 1836—Independence Day—Narcissa Whitman and Eliza Spalding rode over the South Pass of the Rocky Mountains, becoming the first white women to cross the Continental Divide. But this achievement was soon overshadowed by bad news. They learned from some Indians that Rev. Parker would not be meeting them at the Green River Rendezvous. Instead, he had decided to take the long sea route home around South America. He left no instructions about where the Whitmans and Spaldings should establish their missions.

Marcus and Henry made the best of a bad situation and discussed the possibilities with two Nez Perce chiefs. Both the Nez Perces and the Cayuses sought missionaries, but the chiefs warned of possible problems with the Cayuses. Despite the Nez

On July 4, Eliza wrote in her diary, "Crossed a ridge of land today; called the divide, which separates the waters that flow into the Atlantic from those that flow into the Pacific, and camped for the night on the headwaters of the Colorado." Today, this monument at South Pass commemorates the women's accomplishment.

Perces' concerns, the missionaries decided to go to both the Nez Perces and the Cayuses in what is now eastern Washington and western Idaho.

The missionaries left the rendezvous on July 16 with Hudson's Bay Company men and spent the next six weeks traveling the 600 miles or so between the Green River and the Columbia River. They then floated down the Columbia to the Hudson's Bay Company's Fort Vancouver, across the river from present-day Portland, Oregon. On September 12, the missionaries were welcomed by Dr. John McLoughlin, the director of Fort Vancouver. Their journey was nearly over.

Washington before the Whitmans

The region that became the state of Washington had been home to the Nez Perces and other Nez Perce-speaking peoples, including the Cayuse and Walla Walla Indians, for untold generations before Europeans arrived. Fur attracted the Europeans, and the Europeans brought diseases that killed up to 90 percent of the native population by the early 1800s.

The British North West Company (which later merged with the Hudson's Bay Company) and the American-owned Pacific Fur Company competed for control of the fur trade during the War of 1812, but the British won out. Despite Robert Gray's exploration of the Columbia River in 1792 and Lewis and Clark's overland journey to the Northwest in 1805, the area was still dominated by the British in the 1830s.

In 1832, however, Christian newspapers ran a story that sparked missionaries' interest in the Northwest. A delegation of Flathead Indians had gone to St. Louis to request missionaries to come to teach their people about Christianity. A Methodist missionary named Jason Lee went to the Oregon country two years later and started a mission in the Willamette River Valley. Other Protestant missionaries and Catholic priests would not be far behind.

After obtaining supplies from McLoughlin, Whitman and Spalding decided to go to the Nez Perces and the Cayuses to select sites for their missions while the women remained at Fort Vancouver. Narcissa and Eliza enjoyed the legendary hospitality of Dr. McLoughlin. They ate excellent meals and had conversations with educated and worldly company officials.

Meanwhile, Whitman and Spalding were not getting along. Spalding resented Narcissa for spurning his romantic advances many years before, and he envied Marcus. Because of the tensions between the two men, they decided to start separate missions. Whitman would work among the Cayuse Indians, while Spalding concentrated his efforts among the Nez Perces. Whitman decided to open his mission

"What a delightful place," wrote Narcissa Whitman about Fort Vancouver. "What a contrast . . . to the rough barren sand plains through which we have so recently passed."

at Waiilatpu ("place of the rye grass"), near the Hudson's Bay Company's Fort Walla Walla and about seven miles west of present-day Walla Walla, Washington. After searching for a suitable location, Spalding located his mission about 120 miles east, among the Nez Perces at Lapwai ("place of the butterflies"), near today's Spalding, Idaho.

By the time Narcissa arrived in late October, Marcus had started the construction of the mission at Waiilatpu. A large adobe house, gristmill, and blacksmith shop were built in the next few years, but at first Whitman devoted most of his energies to farming and raising livestock.

Narcissa was about four months pregnant when she reached Waiilatpu. On March 14, 1837, she gave birth to a girl, Alice Clarissa Whitman. Alice was a great comfort to Narcissa, who felt lonely and isolated in eastern Washington. Sadly, the child drowned while playing on the banks of the Walla Walla River when she was just two years old.

Efforts by Marcus and Narcissa to convert the Cayuses were, for the most part, futile. There were several reasons for this. For one thing, the Cayuses, like the Nez Perces, were hunter-gatherers who rarely stayed in one place for long. As Spalding once noted in a letter, it was almost impossible to teach people who "were always on the wing." At the same time, the Nez Perce language spoken by the Cayuses was difficult to master, and neither Marcus nor Narcissa was ever able to speak the language well. As a consequence, only a handful of the Indians around the mission ever truly embraced Christianity.

"Where are we now? . . . And who are we that we should be thus blessed of the Lord? I can scarcely realize that we are this comfortably fixed. . . . The house reared & the lean-to enclosed, a good chimney & fireplace & the floor laid."
—Narcissa to her mother, upon arriving at Waiilatpu

Narcissa took solace in her faith when Alice died. "Thy will be done, not mine," she prayed.

They were more successful at convincing the Indians to adopt farming instead of hunting buffalo. The Whitmans also worked to educate the Cayuses, using the written Nez Perce language. In addition, Marcus served as a doctor to the Indians. Practicing medicine on the Cayuses was risky, for the Cayuses believed that if a patient died under medical care, the relatives had the right to kill the doctor.

Personal problems also plagued the missions in the Oregon country. Spalding and Whitman had managed to put aside their differences for the first couple years, but clashes developed as their work became overwhelming. They also had difficulty getting the money or the extra help they needed from

Within a few years, the mission grounds would include a gristmill (at left along the Walla Walla River) and a blacksmith shop (third from left), as well as other outbuildings. The couple's original home was replaced by a large T-shaped house with a parlor, sitting room, kitchen, pantry, an "Indian Room" for the Cayuses, two bedrooms, and a schoolroom.

Reinforcements Rev. Cushing Eells (1810-1893), above, and Rev. Elkanah Walker (1805-1877), below, started a mission among the Spokanes a little more than 20 miles northwest of Spokane, Washington, after their arrival in the Oregon country.

the American Board. When the board finally sent four married couples and another man as "reinforcements" in 1838, the problems increased. Both Whitman and Spalding had trouble getting along with the reinforcements.

Reports of the conflicts at the missions made their way back east. In February 1842, the American Board—financially strapped because of the high cost of mission work and concerned about the difficulties among the missionaries—decided to close both the Waiilatpu and the Lapwai missions.

In September 1842, Whitman received word that the missions were to be closed. Spalding was ordered to return east, while Marcus and Narcissa were to oversee the sale of the mission property and move to a mission near present-day Spokane, which had been founded by two of the missionaries in the reinforcement. Instead of submitting to the decision, Whitman decided to travel east to convince the board to leave the missions open.

Whitman's dedication was remarkable, for the missions were also threatened by Indian hostility at this point. In autumn 1841, a group of Cayuses had suddenly demanded that Whitman pay for the mission land and timber he had used. They threatened to kill him when he pointed out that he had been invited to come. The Indians backed down that time, but tensions were growing. The Cayuses feared that white settlers, who had begun arriving in the region, planned to take their land by force.

On October 3, 1842, Marcus left Narcissa behind at Waiilatpu and departed for the United

States. For the next five months, in mid-winter, he made his way across the wild frontier, arriving at St. Louis in early March 1843. The dangerous journey made him an American hero on par with the mountain men.

To avoid Indian hostilities, Whitman, a guide, and another settler named Asa Lovejoy had taken a much longer southern route. Early winter storms trapped them in the mountains for days at a time. They were forced to eat several of their pack mules and a small dog to avoid starvation. Before crossing

Asa Lovejoy, Marcus's companion, remembered their trek east as "the wildest chase in the world."

One writer described Marcus Whitman's appearance as "the roughest man we have seen this many a day." The American Board in Boston refused to meet with him until he changed into decent clothes.

the Rocky Mountains, Whitman went on ahead to catch up with a party of traders. But he did not find the party and made the rest of the journey alone, vulnerable to Indian attacks in hostile territory. He braved blinding snowstorms and freezing cold weather. When he finally arrived in St. Louis, the exhausted man had a frostbitten nose, toes, and fingers. Dressed in buckskins and a long buffalo coat and sporting a full beard, he made quite an impression. Whitman looked more like a wild mountain man than a doctor-turned-missionary.

Whitman traveled on to Washington, D.C., where he met with the secretary of war and the secretary of state about the Oregon country. The most important part of the trip for him, however, was his meeting with members of the American Board in Boston. In early April 1843, he convinced the board to revoke its orders closing the missions. Waiilatpu would remain open, and Spalding would stay in Oregon on a trial basis.

After spending just a few days in New York with relatives, Whitman had to turn around to start his long trek back to the missions. He joined a huge wagon train that headed out from Missouri in early June 1843 on the Oregon Trail. The first large-scale migration to what was soon to become the Oregon Territory had begun. The wagon train numbered about 1,000 men, women, and children traveling in 120 wagons. On the trek, Whitman worked as a doctor. He delivered babies and treated the sick, but his most important contribution was as a guide.

The Oregon Trail

The Oregon Trail, opened by explorers, fur trappers, traders, and missionaries, was the main route from Missouri to the Northwest during the 1840s and 1850s. Stretching about 2,000 miles between western Missouri and the Columbia River, the trail led thousands of American pioneers to the rich farmland of the Willamette River Valley in the Oregon country. The main trail ran west and then northwest to Fort Kearney in present-day Nebraska. From Fort Kearney, it ran west along the Platte River to Fort Laramie in what is now the state of Wyoming. Leaving Fort Laramie, the trail crossed the South Pass of the Rocky Mountains, then turned southwest to Fort Bridger and finally northwest to Fort Hall near today's Pocatello, Idaho. From Fort Hall, it followed the Snake River to Fort Boise and then led northwest over the Blue Mountains to the Columbia River. Usually the pioneers stopped at Fort Walla Walla, near Waiilatpu, and then went on to Fort Vancouver and the Willamette River Valley.

In 1843 Marcus Whitman helped guide the first large group of settlers along the trail he had traveled in 1836. His description of the West and reports by the Roman Catholic missionary Father Peter De Smet, led to what was known as "Oregon fever." By 1846, about 10,000 men, women, and children had used the trail to cross the continent to the Oregon country. Following the discovery of gold at Sutter's Mill in California in 1848, traffic along the trail slowed as Oregon fever was replaced by gold fever.

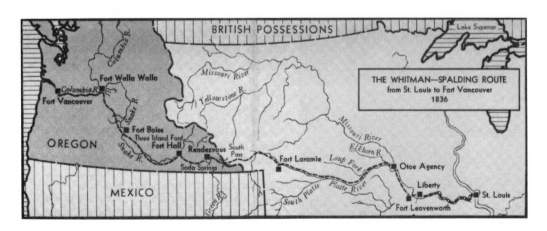

In October 1843, Marcus and Narcissa were finally reunited. Narcissa had spent most of the year at Fort Vancouver and another mission in The Dalles, in what is now eastern Oregon. She was ill when Marcus returned and dreaded returning to the loneliness and endless work of Waiilatpu.

The next few years brought almost constant toil for both Marcus and Narcissa. With all the settlers arriving, between 30 and 60 people were staying at the mission at any one time. And the Whitmans added to the permanent number of residents as well. They had already been taking care of two half Indian girls and an Indian boy. Now the couple adopted seven children, the Sager family, whose parents had died on the Oregon Trail.

These new responsibilities brought the missionary work to a halt. Marcus and Narcissa had to scramble to build extra housing and acquire enough supplies to feed everyone who came through. They still held Sunday worship services for the Indians, but Narcissa's time was now devoted to running a school for the white children. She no longer held classes for the Cayuse boys and girls.

As more settlers arrived, tensions increased with the Cayuses. Some people tried to convince Whitman to leave when confrontations with Indians named Tomahas and Tiloukaikt almost became violent in 1845. John McLoughlin, director of Fort Vancouver, had been influential with the Indians, but he resigned in 1846. When Catholic missionaries arrived in the region at about this time, the Cayuses' suspicions about the Protestants were raised still more. Why did Whitman have any more right to their land than the Catholics did?

Then, in the summer of 1847, measles struck the mission. Most of the whites staying there were ill, but the epidemic was far more devastating among the Cayuses, who had no resistance to the disease. Within weeks, almost half the Cayuse people then living near the mission were dead. Whitman struggled as best he could to stem the epidemic, but he had no more success as a doctor than he'd had as a missionary. Since most of the white people were surviving the disease, the Cayuses now began to fear they were being poisoned to make way for the white settlers from the East. And, as Marcus Whitman well knew, the Cayuses still believed that they had a right to kill a medicine man who failed to cure them.

Located 25 miles west of Waiilatpu, the Hudson's Bay Company's Fort Walla Walla had helped maintain peace in the region. But a new trader had taken charge of the fort in 1846. A Catholic, William McBean failed to curb the Cayuses' discontent with the Protestant missionaries.

Although this illustration from an old biography is not completely accurate, Marcus Whitman was attacked from behind with a tomahawk. He was repeatedly struck in the head and face and then shot in the neck.

There were 75 people, including 45 children, staying at the mission on November 29, 1847. Many of them were bedridden with measles, so Marcus and Narcissa could not flee even though they knew they were in danger. Early that afternoon, a group of Cayuse Indians, led by Tiloukaikt and Tomahas, attacked. Marcus Whitman was one of the first victims of the massacre. By the next day, nine other men had been killed, along with two of the orphan children. Narcissa Whitman had also been murdered, the only female victim of the attack. Forty-six other women and children were taken captive. The captives, with the exception of three children who died of measles, were ransomed one month later by the Hudson's Bay Company.

For all practical purposes, the attack on the Whitman mission spelled an end to the Protestant

missions in the Oregon country. Marcus and Narcissa Whitman's dreams of missionary work in the West had ended in a nightmare. Still, their importance to the opening of the West can hardly be overstated. Together they proved it was possible for women to travel across the Rocky Mountains. The mission they founded served as an important station on the Oregon Trail, providing shelter and help to the thousands of men, women, and children who went on to populate the region that became the states of Washington and Oregon.

The grave of Marcus and Narcissa Whitman at Waiilatpu

Washington after the Whitmans

Even in their deaths, Marcus and Narcissa Whitman served the growth of what became the state of Washington. Although the U.S. government had taken ownership of the Oregon country in 1846, the massacre at Waiilatpu prompted officials to form a government in the region. The Oregon Territory was established in 1848.

Through the 1850s, most of the settlers who followed in the Whitmans' footsteps settled in the Willamette River Valley in Oregon. The settlement of eastern Washington was slowed by a series of Indian wars that broke out in the wake of the massacre at Waiilatpu. Pioneers did establish settlements, however, in western Washington, including Olympia in 1846 and Seattle in 1851.

In early 1853, the U.S. Congress approved the establishment of the Washington Territory. During the next several years, treaties were signed between the United States and the coastal Native Americans, clearing the way for settlement. Agreements came slower with the Cayuses, Nez Perces, and Yakimas in the eastern areas of the territory.

Gold was discovered in northeastern Washington in 1852 and in the Walla Walla area in 1860. The population continued to grow during the next three decades, especially after railroad lines were completed in 1883. There were about 360,000 people living in Washington when it was admitted to the Union as the 42nd state on November 11, 1889.

Chapter Seven

Peter De Smet
and the
Montana and Idaho Missions

O n a summer day in 1821, students in a Catholic school in eastern Flanders (now Belgium) listened intently as a priest pleaded for missionaries to work on the American frontier. "How can it be," the priest asked, "that Napoleon found millions of men ready to sacrifice their lives to ravage a nation and aid him to conquer the world, while I cannot find a handful of devoted men to save an entire people and extend the reign of God?"

One of the young men who took in Father Charles Nerinckx's message that day was 20-year-old Pierre-Jean De Smet. As the priest called for missionary volunteers, Pierre made up his mind. He would go to America—not so much to baptize Indians, but to seek adventure. During the next five decades, he would indeed find adventure, but he also

Peter De Smet (1801-1873), in his old age. The world-traveler for the Roman Catholic faith poses next to a globe with a crucifix in his hand.

discovered his true vocation as a missionary. So much of his life was spent in the United States that he is usually known by the English version of his name, Peter. The Indians he served, however, dubbed him "Black Robe" for his black vestments. This name was renowned throughout the West.

Peter De Smet was born on January 30, 1801, at Termonde, now Dendermonde, in today's Belgium. A twin sister, Collette, followed him into the world a few minutes later. He and his sister were the fifth and sixth of nine children born to Josse-Arnaud De Smet and his wife, Marie-Jeanne. Peter's father owned a company that provided weapons and supplies to military and merchant ships.

A good-looking, athletic boy, Peter earned the nickname "Samson" for his feats of strength and endurance. But he was also interested in books. Even as a teenager, he was able to read not only his native language of Flemish, but also Latin and French. Still, the future missionary was not a very good student and probably worried his father. Perhaps because of concerns about his son's future, Josse De Smet sent him, at the age of 13, to study at a Catholic boarding school in Ghent.

During the next half-dozen years, Peter attended several boarding schools. Then, sometime in 1820, he enrolled at the seminary in Mechelen, near Belgium's current border with the Netherlands. It was there that he heard Father Nerinckx plead for missionaries.

Within days of listening to Nerinckx, Peter volunteered to serve as a missionary. Along with

De Smet's twin sister, Collette, remembered that as a boy, her brother was "a kind of Hercules, a terror to his school fellows, impetuous in the extreme, disputatious, and always in trouble."

five other young men who had also decided to devote their lives to converting the Indians, he set out for Amsterdam to catch a ship for America. After landing in Philadelphia in late September, the missionary recruits settled in at Georgetown College in the District of Columbia. A few weeks later, Peter De Smet began a novitiate in the Roman Catholic order of the Society of Jesus, also called the Jesuits. In White Marsh, Maryland, not far from Washington, D.C., he entered into the lengthy process of education and training that would ultimately lead to his ordination as a Jesuit priest.

For the next six years, De Smet studied logic, metaphysics, philosophy, and theology. The first two years of training were at White Marsh. Then he went to a new novitiate near St. Louis, Missouri. Finally, on September 23, 1827, at the age of 26, he became a priest.

Following his ordination, De Smet began serving as a visiting priest in six small communities within a 150-mile radius of the novitiate in Missouri. He traveled his rounds, on foot and on horseback, from one frontier community to another. On the frontier, De Smet finally met the Indians who had inspired him to come to the United States. Unlike most missionaries at that time, De Smet saw a natural goodness in the Indians.

The Jesuits operated a mission school as part of the novitiate, but financial difficulties forced them to close the school in 1831. De Smet was upset that the Jesuits shut down the mission, for he had come to America to convert the Indians.

Peter tried to hide his decision to go to America as a missionary from his parents. When they found out, they were horrified. Peter's brother Charles was sent to bring him home, but Peter's passion about his plan convinced Charles to donate money instead.

De Smet had a tendency to gain weight, but the rigors of the frontier kept him fit. After describing traveling on horseback and by canoe in a letter to his sister Rosalie, he wrote, "Believe me, this reduces corpulence."

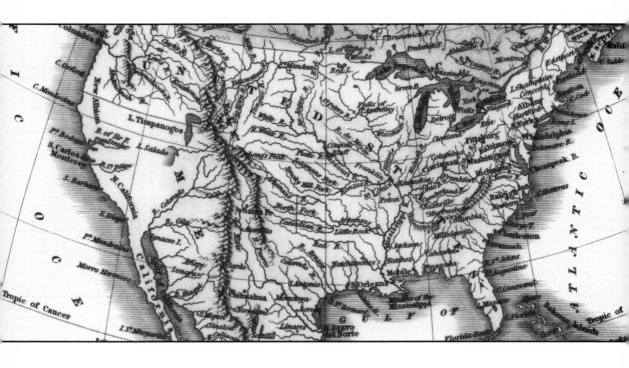

The United States in 1832. The mapmaker drew in the rivers that were crucial for travel in the vast middle of the country when De Smet was first trying to start his missionary work.

Over the next several years De Smet tried unsuccessfully to organize mission expeditions to the Indians living west of Missouri. Each plan fizzled because of a lack of money. In late 1833, the Jesuits decided to send De Smet to Belgium to raise money and attract recruits. The young priest soon proved his worth as a fundraiser, obtaining a substantial amount of cash donations along with mission supplies such as vestments and books.

In November 1834, De Smet and five young Jesuit recruits left Europe for America. But De Smet fell gravely ill during the voyage, apparently from an internal rupture caused by violent vomiting. Too sick to continue, the priest was left with a doctor at the coastal city of Deal, England. During his month of bed rest, De Smet became convinced that he was being punished by God. After all, he had joined the Jesuits more for adventure and excitement than to serve God. Depressed, he decided to leave the Jesuit order but still keep his vows as a priest.

For the next two years, De Smet worked as a priest in a church in Belgium. Through this period, he maintained contact with the Missouri mission and continued to raise money for it. He soon came to feel that his life was incomplete without mission-ary work. Finally, he asked the Society of Jesus to reinstate him. Such a step was almost unheard of, but the head of the order told him he could return.

By late 1837, De Smet was once again in St. Louis. Soon he was chosen to start a mission among the Potawatomi Indians at what is now Council Bluffs, on the western border of the present-day state of Iowa. On May 2, 1838, the priest headed up the Missouri River on a steamboat.

When the ship landed, De Smet wrote, "nearly 2,000 savages in their finest rags and carefully painted in all sorts of patterns" were waiting for them. He had never "seen so imposing a sight nor such fine-looking Indians in America." The Potawatomis, however, were not on hand to greet their new priest. They had come for whiskey.

Alcoholism had already destroyed much of the Potawatomi culture. When they were sober, De Smet found them a gentle people, intelligent and brave. But the whiskey introduced by the whites had done its damage, and De Smet soon had to admit that a mission among the Potawatomis could

When the Potawatomis drank, De Smet wrote, "all their good qualities vanish, they no longer resemble men; all must flee before them; their yells and howls are fearful; they hurl themselves upon each other."

This Flathead delegation went to St. Louis after hearing about Christianity from some Iroquois converts who were traveling with French Canadian fur traders in the region. They believed that the God of the whites might give them the power to survive in a world that was beginning to change all around them.

only fail. He had to find American Indians farther west who had not yet been corrupted by coming into contact with rough fur trappers and unscrupulous traders.

De Smet knew that a group of Flathead Indians had come all the way to St. Louis several times to request missionaries to come to their territory. These Indians had thus far been spared from alcohol abuse, and they were eager to learn about Christianity. De Smet saw his chance and requested permission from his superiors to establish a mission in Flathead territory. In early 1840, his expedition was approved.

De Smet and a Catholic Indian named Young Ignace la Mousse traveled west with an American Fur Company trading caravan. As the caravan made its way across the Great Plains west of Missouri, De Smet fell violently ill, probably from heat exhaustion. The traders urged him to return to Missouri, but he refused to give up. Wracked by fever, the priest rode in the back of a swaying cart, jostled painfully each time the cart hit a rut in the trail.

On June 4, the caravan reached the Laramie River in what is now southeast Wyoming. De Smet had recovered sufficiently to attend a feast at a camp set up by a small party of Cheyenne Indians. De Smet was served a paw, two thighs, and a rack of ribs from a dog slaughtered in his honor. It would be impolite not to eat the meal, so the priest dug in. Fortunately, he found he liked the taste of dog meat.

De Smet and Young Ignace made their way through the Rockies and reached the Green River Rendezvous on June 30. At the gathering of Indians, trappers, and traders, De Smet met a waiting group of Flatheads. The priest rested for a few days and preached to Utes and Shoshones and American trappers. Then he departed for the Flathead camp.

The camp was at a place known as Pierre's Hole on the Snake River in present-day Idaho. About 1,600 Flatheads awaited him. The Flathead chief, Big Face, greeted him warmly. "Black Robe," he said, "welcome to my nation."

For the next two months, De Smet lived with the Flatheads, journeying with them as they searched for game. He converted close to 600 Flatheads and became convinced that a mission with them would meet success. In late August, De Smet announced to Big Face and the other leaders that he had to make his way back to St. Louis before trails were made impassible by winter storms. He promised to return in the spring with more missionaries and supplies.

De Smet left for Missouri on August 27. He and his interpreter met Crows, Mandans, and other Indians and then ran into a large party of Blackfoot Indians near what is now Pierre, South Dakota. When his interpreter introduced him as "the Man Who Talks to the Great Spirit," the Indians carried him into their camp and seated him on a buffalo robe as the guest of honor at a great feast.

Young Ignace's father, also named Ignace, had actually been one of the first Christian missionaries in the Northwest. The elder Ignace, an Iroquois, had been converted by French Jesuits at missions on the St. Lawrence River bordering Canada in the Northeast.

"Black-robe, may the Great Spirit accompany you on your long and dangerous journey. We will offer vows evening and morning that you may arrive safe among your brothers at St. Louis. . . . But when the flowers appear, we will set out to come and meet you. Farewell."
—Big Face, the Flathead chief, to De Smet

Finally, on New Year's Eve, De Smet arrived in St. Louis. He was greeted with bad news. Despite his success, there was no money to finance the missionary expedition. Not deterred, De Smet wrote letters to likely contributors in the East and went on a steamboat down the Mississippi River to solicit funds in person. Within just a few weeks, he raised a total of about $3,000 in cash and collected six crates of supplies for a mission.

De Smet's perseverance paid off. The next July, he and two other Jesuit priests and three Jesuit lay brothers met a group of Flatheads at Green River. (The fur trade had died out, so there was no longer a rendezvous.) They then traveled northwest on the Oregon Trail with a guide and a party of settlers. At Fort Hall, a few miles north of today's Pocatello, Idaho, a large delegation of Flatheads welcomed the party.

Guided by the Flatheads, De Smet's party soon reached the Indians' summer camp. Chief Big Face had already selected a possible site for the Flatheads' permanent village. In De Smet's vision, this village would be the beginning of the Rocky Mountain Mission. The Rocky Mountain Mission would be a series of "reductions"—an old Spanish missionary term for self-sufficient agricultural mission villages. De Smet believed these would give the Indians the strength they needed to withstand the negative influences of American culture that would soon reach them. They would not be dependent on trade with the whites, so they might avoid the ravages alcohol had made in virtually every Indian tribe to the east.

Montana and Idaho before the Missions

For many generations before the first whites came to settle the region we now know as Montana, the area was home to a number of small Indian groups, including the Flatheads, Nez Perces, Kalispels, Shoshones, and Coeur d'Alenes.

In the early 1700s, the Blackfoots, Sioux, Crows, and Cheyennes, who had been displaced from lands farther east, began moving into Montana, pushing the Flatheads, Coeur d'Alenes, and other groups westward, toward the mountains and on into today's Idaho and Washington.

While some traders and trappers visited the region in the middle and late 1700s, the 1805 Lewis and Clark expedition blazed a trail and opened up the region for American settlement.

In 1807, a fur trader named Manuel Lisa established the first trading post in Montana at a site on the Big Horn River in the southeastern part of the state. Lisa's post was soon destroyed by Indians, but British Canadian David Thompson of the North West Company also opened several posts in northwestern Montana and Idaho between 1807 and 1812. Despite Indian resistance, increasing numbers of trappers and traders came into the territory in the first several decades of the 1800s.

Fort Hall, on the Snake River, was founded in 1834 by an American fur trader. Held by the Hudson's Bay Company after 1836, it also became an important station on the Oregon Trail.

The future mission site was on the Bitterroot River, about 30 miles south of present-day Missoula, Montana. They reached it on September 24, 1841. With help from the Flatheads, the Jesuits immediately began building St. Mary's Mission. De Smet, sitting at a desk made of supply crates in a hastily constructed shelter, watched the progress. He could "hear the joyful voices of the carpenters, re-echoing to the blows on the smith's anvil, and I see them engaged in raising the house of prayer."

As the rough-hewn mission took shape, De Smet instructed and converted scores of Indian men, women, and children who lived around St. Mary's. In late October, he and a party of Flatheads journeyed to Fort Colville, a Hudson's Bay Company

"On the first Sunday of October," reported De Smet about the founding of St. Mary's Mission, "we took possession of the promised land by planting a cross on the spot. . . . So many favors have induced us unanimously to proclaim Mary the protectress of our mission, and give her name to it."

outpost on the Columbia River in what is now eastern Washington. He obtained needed supplies there and sent a report to his Jesuit superiors. On that journey, he met members of other Indian groups, especially the Kalispels. Everywhere he went, word of his coming preceded him. He baptized 190 Indians on the trip.

In mid-1842, De Smet set out on another journey, this time to Fort Vancouver, the Hudson's Bay Company base in the Northwest. Again, he was greeted joyously by the Indians, including the Kalispels, Coeur d'Alenes, and Spokanes, as he made his way along the Columbia to the fort at the mouth of the Willamette River.

At Fort Vancouver, De Smet met with two Canadian Catholic missionaries stationed about 20 miles to the south. Inspired by his discussion with them, De Smet began making plans to start the chain of reductions in the Rocky Mountain Mission. There was good reason to make this effort, for De Smet had already converted 1,600 Indians in the Northwest. But to start his mission system, he would need money—lots of money.

So De Smet returned to St. Louis to make use of his fundraising skills again. On his 1843 trip to Europe, De Smet convinced the Pope to appoint a bishop for the Northwest. His efforts to raise money also met with success.

In 1844, De Smet returned to the Northwest with more missionaries and supplies. On that trip, he founded the St. Francis Xavier Mission south of Oregon City on the Willamette River. This mission,

On his trip to Fort Vancouver, De Smet had a brush with death. When his party encountered rough water on the Columbia River, De Smet went ashore and walked along the high bluff. The boat went down in a whirlpool, and five of the eight men on board drowned.

close to Fort Vancouver and the Columbia River, became the main supply center for the Rocky Mountain Mission. De Smet and the other Jesuit missionaries founded six missions in the coming years, including St. Michael's and St. Ignatius in what is now northwestern Idaho; St. Francis Regis, south of Fort Colville on the Columbia River in today's eastern Washington; St. Paul's, north of Fort Colville; and the Sacred Heart Mission on the Spokane River near Lake Coeur d'Alene in Idaho. St. Mary's, the easternmost of the missions, remained the administrative center.

Between 1843 and 1846, De Smet traveled from one mission to another, mostly on foot, covering some 44,000 miles and converting hundreds of Indians. His success was remarkable, since the

Begun in late 1844, the mission of St. Ignatius, named for the founder of the Jesuits, served the Kalispel Indians. A full-scale reduction, St. Ignatius had a cattle ranch and fields of grain.

Protestant missionaries farther west were having severe problems with the Indians. One reason the Indians embraced Catholicism was that De Smet and other Catholics did not try to change all aspects of the Indians' lives. In fact, the Catholics had a policy of adopting at least some local customs and were thus better able to fit in with the Northwest Indians' cultures. Since they did not have to give up their customs, the Indians had little to lose, and they believed they might have much to gain, by adopting Catholicism. For one thing, they thought it would give them strength over their enemies in battle.

But not everything about the missions was a success. De Smet was removed from his post in 1845 because he did not do a good job of managing his subordinate missionaries. He was also criticized

The second of De Smet's reductions, the Sacred Heart Mission among the Coeur d'Alene Indians was founded in November 1842 and moved a year later. The church looked like a small European church.

for starting missions and baptizing Indians without preparing them for a life of Catholic religious observance. The Indians might have converted, but they knew next to nothing about Christian practices.

Unfortunately, De Smet would not have a chance to improve the Rocky Mountain Mission. In November 1847, not long after he settled back into life in St. Louis, Cayuse Indians massacred Marcus and Narcissa Whitman and others at their mission in what is now eastern Washington. The unrest spread, and the Jesuits had to stop building new missions. After years back in the Midwest, De Smet journeyed one last time to the Northwest in 1858 to help the government negotiate peace after the Coeur d'Alene War. He visited his old missions and arranged the peace conference that took place May-June 1859.

From his mission-building days, De Smet (second from right in back row) knew personally the Kalispel, Coeur d'Alene, Colville, and Flathead leaders he posed with at the peace conference in 1859. Their respect for De Smet made them willing to seek peace with the whites.

Montana and Idaho after De Smet

At about the time De Smet left the region, the United States took possession of the Oregon country, which included Montana and Idaho. The American settlement of Montana began in earnest after gold was discovered in 1852. The resulting gold rush brought a large influx of white settlers and led to a decade of wild and woolly action that included stagecoach robberies and shootouts in the streets. The Idaho gold rush started slightly later, after 1860.

During those years, Idaho was first part of the Oregon Territory and then in the Washington Territory. The eastern and western portions of Montana were actually in separate territories. Western Montana was first in the Oregon Territory and then part of the Washington Territory. Eastern Montana was part of Louisiana, then Missouri, Nebraska, and, finally, Dakota. In 1863, the two areas of Montana were joined as part of the Idaho Territory when it was formed. The next year, Montana was made a separate territory.

After the Civil War, cattle ranchers started moving north into Montana from Texas. Conflicts with Indians, particularly the Sioux, increased as whites settled in their territory. In 1876, the Sioux won one of the most famous battles in American history. An American force under the command of George Armstrong Custer was wiped out by the Sioux at the Battle of the Little Big Horn in Montana. In the wake of this battle, however, the Indians of Montana were rounded up by U.S. government forces and removed to reservations.

The Nez Perces in Idaho tried to flee to Canada instead of being forced onto reservations in this period. But they, too, failed. Despite years of negotiations, numerous treaties, and repeated battles for the right to their land, Chief Joseph and the Nez Perces were defeated in 1877.

In the 1880s, when railroads first began serving Montana and Idaho, white settlers came in growing numbers. Sheep and cattle ranchers fought over land rights, farmers planted crops, and more miners came after the discovery of silver and copper.

By the mid-1880s, citizens of Montana were petitioning Congress to make the territory a state. On November 8, 1889, their appeals paid off, and Montana entered the Union as the the 41st state. Idaho became the 43rd state on July 3, 1890.

De Smet's efforts for peace had started on his way back to St. Louis in 1846, when he negotiated a peace treaty between the Flatheads and their long-time enemies, the Blackfoot Indians. This work as a mediator would characterize De Smet's relations with Indians from then on. Practically alone among whites of his time, De Smet lobbied to end the destruction of the buffalo by whites and argued that white settlers should be kept out of the Great Plains.

The priest grew increasingly dismayed by the plight of the Great Plains Indians in the 1850s and 1860s. Even though the government had officially recognized the Indians' titles to lands in treaty negotiations in 1851, it later did nothing to protect the Indians' right to these lands. De Smet had drawn the map showing the tribal boundaries at these negotiations, so he was painfully aware of the injustices.

"When the savages raise the hatchet to go on the warpath, it is because they are pushed to the limit of endurance," wrote De Smet in 1867. "It is always true that if the savages sin against the whites it is because the whites have greatly sinned against them."

When violence broke out between settlers and the Plains Indians in the 1860s, De Smet was not surprised. He believed the government had pushed the Sioux to this extreme, and he openly criticized the government's broken promises. Yet De Smet managed to negotiate a temporary peace between the Indians and the whites in 1868, when he visited the camp of Sitting Bull and convinced the leader to send representatives to meet with the government. The Fort Laramie Treaty granted South Dakota to the Indians. This treaty, too, would soon be broken.

By the late 1860s, De Smet was beginning to tire. Following the peace conference in 1868, he was ordered by his superiors to go once again to Europe for medical care. After spending as much of

his time in Europe raising money as recuperating, De Smet returned to America. In mid-1870, he traveled up the Missouri River in search of a site for a mission to serve the Indians of the northern plains. This trip was his last to the Indian country.

On May 23, 1873, Peter De Smet died in his sleep in his room at St. Louis University, the school that grew out of the Jesuit novitiate he had attended a half century earlier. Thousands of people went to his funeral. De Smet's lifetime achievements as a fundraiser, missionary, and peacemaker were remarkable. He had served the Indians in the ways he thought best: defending their way of life, negotiating peace, and converting thousands of Indians throughout the Northwest and the Great Plains.

When De Smet (sitting in the black robe) approached Sitting Bull about making peace, Sitting Bull responded, "I will listen to thy good words, and as bad as I have been to the whites, just so good am I ready to become toward them."

Chapter Eight

Brigham Young
and the
Mormon Zion of Utah

I n the summer of 1847, a wagon halted atop a hill overlooking a desolate valley. A man looked out from the back of the wagon and gazed westward over the land below. After several moments, he spoke. "This is the place," he told his wagon driver.

With those few words, 46-year-old Brigham Young laid claim to the Salt Lake Valley in Utah. The leader of the Church of Jesus Christ of Latter-day Saints, also known as the Mormon Church, he was about to lead the largest migration in American history. Young was planning the move of about 20,000 Mormons to the region. For the next three decades, he would oversee the building of what the Mormons called the state of Deseret. From its capital of Salt Lake City, Young and his followers would establish a worldwide church.

Brigham Young (1801-1877), patriarch of Mormonism and father of Utah, late in his life

Born on June 1, 1801, in Whitingham, Vermont, Brigham was the ninth of John and Abigail Young's eleven children. The Youngs were poor and moved frequently in search of better work. When Brigham was three years old, the family relocated to western New York, an area often called the "burned-over district" because of all the religious revivals there in the late 1700s and early 1800s. Brigham spent most of his boyhood working to help feed the family. Although he had only two months of schooling, he learned about the Bible from his mother and father, who were devout Methodists.

Abigail Young died from tuberculosis in June 1815, when Brigham was 14. The teenager left home two years later when his father remarried. He apprenticed as a carpenter in Auburn, New York, and worked there for the next six years. In 1823, Brigham met 17-year-old Miriam Works, who was from the neighboring town of Port Byron. Within a year, they were married.

At about the time that Brigham Young met Miriam Works, a neighbor described him as a good-looking man, "as fine a specimen of young manhood as I have ever known." He was close to six feet tall and muscular, with blond hair and blue eyes.

For the next several years, it appeared that Brigham's life would parallel his father's. Miriam fell ill with the same disease that had killed Brigham's mother. Impoverished, Brigham moved from town to town in search of work as a laborer and carpenter. His young family was often on the brink of starvation. Brigham, also like his father, tried to find solace in religion.

Then Brigham Young discovered Mormonism. Within months of Joseph Smith's publication of the Book of Mormon in March 1830, a copy was making the rounds in the Young family.

According to Mormon beliefs, Joseph Smith, a farmer, was led by an angel to golden tablets buried on a hillside near Palmyra, New York. In writing that looked like Egyptian hieroglyphics, the tablets told the story of an ancient people who had come to the New World from Palestine 600 years before the birth of Jesus Christ. Smith translated the story on the tablets, publishing it as the Book of Mormon. In 1830, the Church of Jesus Christ of Latter-day Saints was officially formed. Its doctrines were based on the Bible, the Book of Mormon, and revelations received by Joseph Smith. To Mormons, Smith was a prophet as well as their founder and president.

Joseph Smith (1805-1844) was only 25 years old when he founded the Mormon Church, which now has almost 5 million members in the United States alone.

The Mormons offered what Brigham viewed as a "pure" form of Christianity. They preached good deeds and absolute obedience to the church and its leaders. Particularly attractive to Brigham was Smith's promise that he would build God's kingdom on Earth for his followers. All Mormon men could become priests and rise to positions of power. While Brigham had flirted with many religions throughout his life, Mormonism made sense to him.

Phinehas Young, one of Brigham's brothers, was the first convert in the family. Another brother and Brigham's father followed. On April 14, 1832, Brigham Young stepped into a shallow creek behind his house in Mendon, New York, and was baptized into the Mormon Church. The rest of the Young family were soon also members of the church.

In September 1832, Miriam, herself a recent convert, died of tuberculosis. Brigham was left with two young daughters to raise. A month after his

"I used to go to meetings—was well acquainted with the Episcopalians, Presbyterians, New Lights, Baptists, Freewill Baptists, Wesleyan and Reform Methodists . . . —and was more or less acquainted with almost every other religious ism."
—Brigham Young, on his early search for religion

wife's death, Brigham traveled to Kirtland, Ohio—one of several thriving Mormon communities—to meet with Joseph Smith. This meeting convinced Young that Smith was a prophet. From then on, Brigham devoted himself to Mormonism. He traveled in Canada, New England, and New York as a missionary. After moving to Kirtland in September 1833, he helped build homes and a temple.

Brigham was rewarded for his devotion. In February 1835, he was named one of the Council of the Twelve Apostles, a church committee second in power only to Smith himself. Young held the top position in the Twelve by 1838.

After their temple in Kirtland, Ohio, was completed, the Mormons held a dedication ceremony in which Smith washed the feet of Young and the other members of the Twelve, as Jesus had washed the feet of his apostles.

As the growing church founded new settlements, it was rocked by conflicts, especially between Saints, as Mormons called themselves, and Gentiles (non-Mormons). Gentiles beat Saints in Independence, Missouri, more than once. Problems were also arising within the church over Smith's handling of money.

So many Mormons quit the church and turned against the founder that Smith and Young fled from Kirtland to Far West, a Mormon community in Missouri in the winter of 1837-1838. One year later, Young led the Missouri Mormons to Illinois. Smith was jailed in Missouri in 1839 for his beliefs, but he escaped and made his way to Illinois, where he founded the town of Nauvoo, Illinois. Through all this turmoil, Young's faith was unswerving. Along with the rest of the Council of Twelve, he traveled to England in the spring of 1840 and convinced thousands of converts to emigrate to the United States.

Then his faith was rocked. In 1841, Smith revealed to the Twelve the controversial Mormon doctrine of plural marriage. The great biblical leaders of the Old Testament had several wives, and Smith now concluded that Mormon men should follow the practice of their biblical forebears. Most

The ordination of Joseph Smith and Oliver Cowdery by John the Baptist. Oliver Cowdery was one of only three people who saw Joseph Smith's golden tablets.

non-Mormons believed plural marriage, commonly known as polygamy, was sinful and illegal.

Brigham Young had wed a Mormon woman named Mary Ann Angell in 1834. When Smith introduced the doctrine of plural marriage to Young, he told him to take a second wife. Brigham was dismayed. "I was not desirous of shirking from any duty," he later said, "nor of failing in the least to do as I was commanded, but it was the first time in my life that I had desired the grave." He wanted to obey Smith, but he had serious doubts about the morality of plural marriages. Finally, his faith that Smith was preaching the word of God won out.

In June 1842, Young married his first plural wife, Lucy Ann Decker Seeley. He married three more times in the next two years and then added 15 more wives by May 1845 and another 18 by February 1846. Brigham Young would marry a total of 55 women.

As more Mormons embraced polygamy, the practice became difficult to hide from prying outsiders. Many Mormons had left the church over the issue and turned against their old leaders. In early 1844, the conflicts between the Mormons and Gentiles came to a head, and Smith realized they would have to move to someplace more isolated.

But moving the entire group of Mormons was beyond the financial capacity of the church. Hoping to gain more converts and win public sympathy for their plight, Smith decided to seek election as president of the United States. On May 21, 1844, Young left Nauvoo on a campaign tour for Smith.

"There is not a single constitution of any single state much the less the constitution of the federal government, that hinders a man from having two wives; and I defy all the lawyers of the United States to prove to the contrary."
—Young, on polygamy

144

Soon after Young's departure, a group of dissident Mormons published a newspaper to air their complaints. Enraged, Smith's followers stormed the newspaper office, smashing the printing press and destroying unsold copies of the paper. After that attack, Joseph Smith and his brother Hyrum were arrested and jailed in Carthage, Illinois, not far from Nauvoo. On June 27, the jail was overrun by a mob. Both Joseph and Hyrum Smith were shot to death.

Brigham Young did not learn of the murders until July 16. He rushed back to Nauvoo to find the Mormon Church in chaos. Acting quickly, he organized a meeting of the church. On August 8, at that meeting, the Mormons determined that the "mantle of the Prophet" was on Young's shoulders.

Harper's Weekly, *a popular magazine, mocked Young's "harem," as it termed his family. Young would have 57 children by his wives, but he also married many widows simply to provide for them financially.*

It was the Nauvoo Temple that kept Young in Illinois so long. He believed its completion was crucial to the Mormon faith and its ceremonies.

Still, the Mormons were not united behind Young. In addition, Mormons were at the mercy of mob violence, suffering assaults and rapes. Young assumed near-dictatorial powers to respond to the crises. He kicked troublemakers out of the church, and the men of Nauvoo organized a militia and a police force as the Mormons prepared for the worst.

In the face of growing anti-Mormon feeling, the Illinois state legislature revoked the charter of the city of Nauvoo in January 1845. Young now saw that the Mormons would once again be forced to move. Soon, he was planning an exodus to the recently explored valley of the Great Salt Lake. To Young, the desolate valley in what is today the state of Utah was ideal. Uninhabited by white settlers, it was secluded and remote. Since much of its land was barren, he thought non-Mormons would leave his people in peace.

The mass migration of some 20,000 Mormon faithful from Illinois and other communities was a vast undertaking. Young planned and supervised every stage of the move. He determined that each family of five should travel in a wagon drawn by six oxen. Groups of 50 families would travel together for safety. He even gave orders about the amounts of supplies for each wagon.

In February 1846, several hundred Mormons departed from Nauvoo and crossed the Mississippi River into eastern Iowa, where they set up temporary camps. By mid-May, more than 10,000 had gathered. Traveling along 300 miles of roads muddy from spring rains, the groups reached the eastern edge of the Nebraska Territory in mid-June. There Young established a settlement known as Winter Quarters. The Mormons planted crops and prepared to wait out the winter.

The winter was difficult, and many Mormons, including two of Brigham's wives, fell ill and died. Brigham himself was sick most of the winter. Nevertheless, Young prepared an advance group to head west in the spring in preparation for the huge migration. With a group of 143 men, 3 women, and 2 children, Young departed from Winter Quarters in April 1847.

Following a grueling schedule, the Mormons made their way to Fort Kearney, Nebraska, where they joined the Oregon Trail. They followed the Platte River across Nebraska and into Wyoming and crossed the Rocky Mountains over the South Pass. At Fort Bridger, they turned southwest from the Oregon Trail and crossed the Wasatch Mountains, entering what would become the state of Utah. They had covered 1,031 miles in just 111 days.

Finally, in July 1847, a small party entered the Salt Lake Valley. Young, who was ill, followed several days behind in a wagon driven by his friend Wilford Woodruff. On July 24, 1847, Young looked down on the valley he hoped would be a safe haven.

The advance group of 1847 traveled like an army. Each day a bugle woke the company at 5 A.M. Travel began at about 7:30 A.M. and continued until about 6:30 P.M. After prayers and an evening meal, the Mormons retired at 9 P.M. This strict schedule enabled the wagon train to travel about 10 miles a day.

Utah before the Mormons

Utah was home to a rich Indian culture long before Europeans developed cities. The ancestors of the Basket-makers inhabited southern Utah by about 4,000 years ago and developed fine basket-making and extensive agriculture over a period of several thousand years. Their descendants were the Pueblo Indians, whose homes, hewn into the cliffs of the region, can still be found in southeastern Utah. The Pueblos were later joined by the Paiutes, who were hunter-gatherers, and the hostile Navajos, who raided the Pueblo Indians. The Utes dominated the area in the mid-1800s. Northern Utah was part of the range of the Shoshone Indians, who hunted buffalo.

Thanks to its isolated location, Utah was left untouched for many years after European settlements were thriving along the Atlantic and Pacific coasts. The first Europeans who are known to have entered Utah were Spanish missionaries, Silvestre Vélez de Escalante and Francisco Atanasio Dominguez in 1776. They were mapping a route between Santa Fe, New Mexico, and the missions established by Junípero Serra and other Franciscans in California.

Although the United States recognized Utah as Mexican territory, by the 1820s American trappers were searching for pelts in the region. But the beaver were soon depleted and the area remained mostly unknown to Americans or Mexicans.

That began to change in 1841 when a party of emigrants passed through Utah on the way to California. John C. Frémont made the first scientific survey of the huge Great Basin region two years later. By the mid-1840s, pioneer Miles Goodyear had established a fort in Ogden, Utah. But the area was mostly uninhabited by Americans when the Mormons were seeking sanctuary.

John C. Frémont (1824-1902) was called the "Pathfinder" because he opened so many trails in the West.

By the time Young entered the valley, the men traveling ahead had already planted five acres of potatoes. Others prepared to go in search of timber, water, and grass for grazing. "You will find many excellent places for settlement," Young told them. "This is the place which the Lord has chosen for us to commence our settlements, and from this place we shall spread abroad and possess the land." Those words were truly prophetic.

Within days, the Mormon Zion was being built. Streets 132 feet wide formed square blocks of 10 acres each. Each block was divided into eight lots, and houses were staggered so those on opposite sides of a street would not face each other. Water diverted for irrigation from a creek north of town flowed along ditches on both sides of each street.

Salt Lake City after 20 years of Mormon development. The brand-new Tabernacle, seating 15,000, is the rounded building toward the right, next to the unfinished Temple.

With the work underway, Young and many of the rest started back to Winter Quarters to prepare the waiting Saints for migration the next year. Once there, the Twelve turned their attention to church government. On December 5, 1847, Brigham Young was formally elected the second president of the church. Young appointed two others as his closest advisors. The three men together formed the new "First Presidency," the church's highest body.

Young fulfilled his role well. The great migration of 1848 went smoothly, and 5,000 Mormons were settling into the Salt Lake Valley by September 1848. More would come the next year. The territory became part of the United States that year, as well, with the signing of the Treaty of Guadalupe Hidalgo with Mexico. Young continually enlarged the Mormon holdings, sending groups of Mormons to build other settlements in fertile valleys.

Pioneers on the Mormon Trail. On the trek west, a Mormon invented a machine that could be used to measure distance traveled. This machine, built by "fixing a set of wooden cog wheels to the hub of a wagon wheel," was the first known odometer.

Young sent missionaries around the world to convert more people. The church then provided wagons and teams of oxen so these converts could come to Deseret. Young created a fund to lend money to needy immigrants, and once they arrived they were given temporary employment. In addition, Young established a system of industries so that Mormon communities could be self-sufficient.

Young began seeking statehood for Deseret in 1849. The U.S. Congress organized the region as the Utah Territory in 1850, with Young as governor, but Young kept trying to get the increased independence of statehood. By 1852, there were 30,000 Mormons in Utah. Three years later that number had doubled to 60,000. During the following years, Young oversaw the establishment of some 325 settlements and towns, stretching across what is now Utah, Idaho, Nevada, Arizona, and California.

While Utah and the Church of Jesus Christ of Latter-day Saints were growing, trouble was brewing. Beginning in summer 1853, Mormons suffered a year-long rash of attacks by Ute Indians, losing hundreds of livestock and forestalling the spread of new settlements. That same year, President Franklin Pierce threatened to remove Young as governor. Then, in 1856, a drought was followed by an invasion of crop-hungry locusts. Livestock starved to death, and people went hungry.

The church could no longer afford to provide immigrants with wagons and oxen teams. Young now ordered them to carry their belongings on two-wheeled handcarts that they would push or pull

Deseret was a huge territory, stretching all the way from Mexico to Oregon and from the Rocky Mountains on the east to the Sierra Nevada on the west. It took its name from a word in the Book of Mormon meaning "honeybee" to represent Mormon industriousness.

When President Franklin Pierce (above) threatened to appoint a new governor, Young was defiant. "I am and will be governor," he declared, "and no power can hinder it, until the Lord Almighty says, 'Brigham, you need not be governor any longer.'"

James Buchanan had been president only a few months when he sent troops to Utah. He took a much more hostile stance than previous presidents due to overwhelming pressure from people opposed to Mormons.

along. "If it is once tried, you will find that it will become the favorite mode of crossing the plains," Young wrote in the *Millennial Star*, a Mormon magazine. "I should not be surprised if a company of this kind should make the trip in sixty or seventy days."

For a time, it appeared that Young was right. Several groups of migrants safely made the trek from eastern Iowa to Utah pushing brightly painted carts. Then tragedy struck. Handcart migrants were trapped in a winter storm, and 200 perished.

Brigham viewed the famine and the handcart tragedy as punishment from God. Mormon leaders started what they called the "Reformation" to rekindle devotion to the faith. Unfortunately, rumors twisted the Reformation. Anti-Mormons claimed a group called "Danites"—angels of vengeance—was committing murders of Mormon sinners in Utah. In 1857, word of the supposed atrocities and rumors that Mormons were defying the laws and authority of the United States added to furor over Mormon polygamy. President James Buchanan removed Young from his post as territorial governor. He also ordered U.S. Army troops in to stop what he thought might be the start of an armed rebellion.

Early in September 1857, in the midst of this crisis, a large wagon train was heading to California through southern Utah. The Indians there believed the pioneers had poisoned them, and the Mormons feared the group was part of a government invasion. When the Indians asked the Mormons to help them attack the wagon train, the Mormons sent a messenger to Brigham Young to ask for guidance. His response came too late. On September 11, 1857, a group of Indians and Mormons attacked the pioneers at Mountain Meadows in southwestern Utah. About 120 men, women, and children were killed in the Mountain Meadows Massacre. Only 18 small children were spared.

Young wept when he heard about the massacre. But he was told that only the Indians had taken part, and he did not learn the full horror of the Mormon involvement until months later. When the U.S. Army invaded Utah shortly after the tragedy, Young decided it would be better to avoid bloodshed. Reluctantly, the Mormons accepted their newly appointed governor. Young and other Mormons were pardoned in June 1858 for the massacre and other offenses.

"In regard to the emigration trains passing through our settlements, we must not interfere with them . . . . You should try to preserve good feelings with them."
—Young's message to the Mormons in southern Utah, September 10, 1857, one day before the massacre

Only one Mormon, John D. Lee, was ever convicted and executed for his part in the massacre. Young eventually excommunicated Lee from the church and allowed him to take the punishment for all the Mormon participants.

In addition to problems with the government, conflicts between white settlers and the Utes worsened. The late 1860s brought numerous attacks by the Utes on outlying Mormon settlements. In 1868, the Utes were finally vanquished.

Both Utah and the Mormon Church evolved in this period. After the discovery of silver in 1859 brought many non-Mormons into the territory, the Mormons adopted some of the customs they are known for today. Based on a revelation Joseph Smith had recorded, but perhaps also in reaction to the hard-drinking miners entering the region, Brigham Young began to promote abstinence from tobacco, alcohol, coffee, and tea in the 1860s. Young was not opposed to the modern world, however, and

Brigham Young's estate in Salt Lake City in 1862. Young's official residence was the Beehive House (center, with cupola), where his favored wife lived as well. Most of his wives and children lived at Lion House (the large building with two chimneys toward the left). His children went to school in the building on the right.

he pushed for the completion of the transcontinental telegraph line and railroad line in the 1860s.

For the rest of his life, Brigham Young remained embroiled in seemingly endless battles with the U.S. government over the issues of plural marriage and Mormon self-rule. Repeatedly, the new governor accused Young of treason, and polygamy blocked Utah's quest for statehood. In autumn 1871, Young was arrested for his plural marriages and for allegedly ordering a murder in revenge for anti-Mormon acts. Both charges were later dropped.

By 1873, age and chronic health problems forced Young into partial retirement. One summer evening in 1877, he complained of feeling ill and went to bed. Six days later, on the 29th of August, Young opened his eyes and gazed upward as if at a vision. "Joseph!" he cried, calling the name of his friend the prophet Joseph Smith. "Joseph! Joseph! Joseph!" he called again. Then, with a gasp, he died.

To his critics, Brigham Young was a tyrant and rogue. To his followers, he was the savior of Mormonism. But it cannot be denied that the massive migration of Mormons to Utah was without parallel in the history of the United States.

This monument to Joseph Smith, the founder of Mormonism, stands on Temple Square in Salt Lake City.

Utah from Territory to Statehood

There were more than 100,000 people in Utah by the time Brigham Young died in 1877, many of whom were non-Mormons attracted by the mining boom. In 1890, Wilford Woodruff, fourth president of the Mormon Church, realized the Mormons must renounce polygamy in order to join the United States. Six years later, Congress approved Utah's request to become a state, and it entered the Union as the 45th state on January 4, 1896.

Utah is still the stronghold of the Mormon religion, but there are many Mormons in other states. Effective missionaries, Mormons have spread their religion all over the world and are no longer a persecuted minority.

Wilford Woodruff (1807-1898), longtime friend of Brigham Young

Mining in Colorado, Utah, and Nevada

Unfortunately for the Mormons, the rich mineral resources of the Utah Territory, including Nevada and part of Colorado, enticed miners. The Mormons managed to delay mining in what is today Utah proper until the mid-1860s, but copper is now one of Utah's greatest resources. Gold, silver, and copper mining fueled explosive population growth in Colorado, Utah, Nevada, Idaho, Montana, and California. Miners founded hundreds of boomtowns near mining strikes.

Settlers seeking California gold went through what is now Nevada from 1849 on, and Mormons began to spread out into Nevada from their base in Salt Lake City. But by the time gold was found in 1859, Mormons had retreated back to Utah because of conflicts with the U.S. government. Miners came in hordes to Nevada, even leaving California to dig at the fabulous Comstock Lode for silver in the mountains of western Nevada. Dozens of boomtowns sprung up, and Nevada became a territory in 1861 to provide some law and order. It became a state three years later with its capital at Carson City in the middle of the silver-mining region. Nevada's mineral wealth remains rich to this day, an industry second only to the state's huge gambling industry.

Desire for gold brought the first European explorers to what is now southwestern Colorado as well. Spaniards coming north from Mexico in the mid-1700s hoped to find the gold that had enriched their forebears in Mexico and South America. Except for fur trappers and later missionaries, Americans showed little interest in Colorado until the great mining strikes of the mid-1800s. Gold was discovered at Cherry Creek, near what is now Denver in 1858 and at Central City west of Denver the next year, bringing a flood of miners. Colorado became a territory in 1861, with its population concentrated by the gold fields in the Denver area. Statehood was harder to achieve, however, and the gold mines petered out by the mid-1860s. In the 1870s, a new mining boom started after the discovery of silver-bearing ore near Leadville in the mountains. Spurred by mining growth, Colorado finally became a state in 1876.

Leadville, Colorado, in its silver-mining heyday. The lead had silver in it, and 40,000 people had moved there to look for it by 1880. Now Leadville's population has dwindled to less than 4,000.

A Western Timeline

October 12, 1492: Christopher Columbus lands in the West Indies, opening New World colonization for Spain.

1528-1536: Álvar Nuñez Cabeza de Vaca leads a group of explorers through parts of the Southwest.

1540-1542: Francisco Vásquez de Coronado enters New Mexico and Arizona in his search for the Seven Cities of Cibola.

1542: A Portuguese explorer, Juan Rodríguez Cabrillo, sails the coast of California under the Spanish flag.

1552: **Juan de Oñate** is born in Zacatecas, Mexico.

1579: Sir Francis Drake lands in northern California, claiming the region for England.

September 21, 1595: **Oñate** receives a commission to take New Mexico.

April 30, 1598: **Oñate** claims New Mexico for Spain.

July 11, 1598: **Oñate**'s party reaches the site of their first settlement, near today's Espanola, New Mexico.

December 1, 1598: A party of **Oñate**'s men is attacked by the Ácoma Indians.

January 1599: Vicente de Zaldívar and the Spaniards crush the Ácoma uprising.

1599 or 1600: **Oñate** moves his settlement across the Rio Grande and founds San Gabriel by taking over another pueblo.

June-November 1601: **Oñate** searches for Quivira, a city of gold, traveling as far as present-day Kansas.

June-November 1601: The Spanish colonists abandon San Gabriel and flee to Mexico while **Oñate** is gone.

1602-1603: Spaniard Sebastian Vizcaíno leads an expedition to California.

January 1605: **Oñate** reaches the Gulf of California overland.

August 24, 1607: **Oñate** resigns his commission to colonize New Mexico.

1607 or 1608: The remaining Spaniards in New Mexico move to a new site that will become Santa Fe, New Mexico.

1610: Santa Fe is officially founded by Pedro de Peralta, **Oñate**'s successor.

May 1614: Spanish authorities find **Oñate** guilty of 12 charges of mismanagement of the New Mexico colony and mistreatment of the Indians there.

June 3, 1626: **Oñate** dies in Spain at the age of about 74.

August 10, 1645: Eusebio Kino is born in the village of Segno in what is now Italy.

Autumn 1665: **Kino** enters the Jesuit order as a novice; he becomes a priest in 1677.

1680: The Indians of the San Juan pueblo rise against the Spaniards, driving them from New Mexico.

January 27, 1681: **Kino** leaves Europe for Mexico to start his missionary work.

April 2, 1683: **Kino** is part of an expedition to claim Baja California for Spain.

Mid-July 1683: The Spanish flee Baja California because of Indian hostilities.

Spring 1687: Kino is sent to the Pimería Alta, in today's northern Mexico and southern Arizona, to build missions.

Spring 1687: Kino founds Nuestra Señora de los Dolores in Sonora, Mexico, his headquarters for his work in Sonora and Arizona.

1691-1692: Kino establishes three missions in southern Arizona.

1702: Kino proves that Baja California is a peninsula, not an island.

March 15, 1711: Kino dies at the age of 65 at Mission Magdalena in Sonora, Mexico, one of his many settlements.

November 24, 1713: Junípero Serra is born in Petra on the island of Majorca in the Mediterranean Sea.

September 14, 1730: Serra joins the Franciscan order; he becomes a priest in 1737.

August 30, 1749: Serra leaves Spain for Mexico to become a missionary.

July 1767: After the Jesuits are banished from Spanish territories in the New World, **Serra** takes over their missions in Baja California.

July 16, 1769: Serra founds Mission San Diego in today's San Diego, the first permanent European settlement in California.

June 3, 1770: Serra establishes Mission San Carlos in present-day Carmel; it will become his headquarters.

1770s: Juan Bautista de Anza and Father F. T. H. Garcés establish missions in southwest Arizona.

1775: A Spanish party lands on the coast of Washington or Oregon.

1776: Spanish missionaries Silvestre Vélez de Escalante and Francisco Atanasio Dominguez map a route from Santa Fe, New Mexico, through Utah and Nevada to the Spanish missions in California.

January 20, 1778: Captain James Cook of England is the first European to land on the Hawaiian Islands.

March 1778: Captain Cook arrives in the Pacific Northwest.

1784: Russian traders found their first settlement in Alaska on Kodiak Island.

August 28, 1784: Serra dies at Mission San Carlos at the age of 70.

October 19, 1784: John McLoughlin is born in what is now Quebec, Canada.

May 11, 1792: American Robert Gray sails up the Columbia River, laying claim to the area.

1792: British George Vancouver explores the Washington and Oregon coastline and makes the first maps of the region.

January 30, 1801: Peter De Smet is born in today's Dendermonde, Belgium.

June 1, 1801: Brigham Young is born in Whitingham, Vermont.

September 4, 1802: Marcus Whitman is born near Rushville, New York.

February 15, 1803: John Sutter is born in Kandern in present-day Germany.

April 30, 1803: Through the Louisiana Purchase, the United States acquires much of the interior of North America.

1804: McLoughlin begins working for the British North West Company in Canada as a physician and fur trader.

1804-1805: Meriwether Lewis and William Clark, leading the Corps of Discovery, open an overland route to the Northwest as they seek a water route through the North American continent.

1807: Manuel Lisa establishes the first fur-trading post in Montana.

March 14, 1808: Narcissa Whitman is born in Prattsburg, New York.

1811: John Jacob Astor's Pacific Fur Company founds Astoria, Oregon.

1812: Russian fur traders establish two forts on the California coast.

1813: The British North West Company takes Astoria and renames it Fort George.

1818: The United States and England agree to joint occupancy of the Northwest.

Summer 1820: De Smet decides to become a Jesuit missionary in the United States; he becomes a priest in 1827.

August 24, 1821: Mexico wins independence from Spain and takes control of Spanish territories in North America.

1821: The British fur-trading companies the North West Company and Hudson's Bay Company decide to merge, keeping the Hudson's Bay name.

1822: Using the Santa Fe Trail linking Independence, Missouri, with Santa Fe, New Mexico, American traders begin coming to New Mexico.

1824: Mountain man Jedediah Smith finds an easy route through the South Pass of the Rocky Mountains.

November 8, 1824: To oversee the Columbia River region, **McLoughlin** takes over the Hudson's Bay Company post of Fort George in today's Astoria, Oregon.

March 19, 1825: McLoughlin officially founds the new Fort Vancouver at the site of Vancouver, Washington.

1826: Mountain man Jedediah Smith leads a party overland into California.

1828: McLoughlin explores and claims land on the falls of the Willamette River, the future site of Oregon City, Oregon.

1830: Joseph Smith founds the Church of Jesus Christ of Latter-day Saints, or the Mormon Church.

April 14, 1832: Young converts to the Mormon religion.

May 1834: Sutter leaves Switzerland for the United States.

1834: American Methodist missionaries first arrive in the Northwest.

November 1834: Marcus and **Narcissa Whitman** respond to a call for missionaries to the Northwest Indians.

August 1835: Marcus Whitman meets with Flathead and Nez Perce Indians seeking missionaries at the Green River Rendezvous in Wyoming.

May 1836: With another missionary couple, **Marcus** and **Narcissa Whitman** head west from Missouri for Oregon.

July 4, 1836: Narcissa Whitman and Eliza Spalding are the first white women to cross the Continental Divide.

July 1836: Marcus Whitman and Henry Spalding decide to go to the Nez Perces and the Cayuses after meeting with two Nez Perce chiefs near Green River.

September 12, 1836: The **Whitmans** and their party are greeted by **John McLoughlin** at Fort Vancouver on the Columbia River.

October 1836: Whitman founds Waiilatpu near Walla Walla, Washington.

Spring 1838: Sutter heads west for Mexican California.

August 1838: More missionaries arrive to aid the **Whitmans** and the Spaldings in the Oregon country.

July 1, 1839: Sutter arrives in Yerba Buena (later San Francisco), California.

August 13, 1839: Sutter reaches the future site of Sacramento, California.

Early 1840: De Smet is allowed to start a mission among the Flathead Indians.

July 1840: De Smet arrives at the Flathead camp at Pierre's Hole, Idaho, and makes plans with them to start a mission.

August 1840: Sutter receives a grant for his land from the Mexican government.

October 8, 1840: Hawaii establishes a constitutional monarchy. Americans soon become involved in the government.

September 24, 1841: De Smet founds St. Mary's Mission, south of today's Missoula, Montana. It becomes the headquarters of his Rocky Mountain Mission.

October 1841: The Hudson's Bay Company governor closes several of **McLoughlin**'s forts.

1841: The first overland wagon trains travel from the United States to California and the Oregon country.

September 1842: Whitman learns that the missionary board has decided to close the Oregon missions.

October 3, 1842: Whitman sets out east to convince the board to keep the missions open.

1843: Captain John C. Frémont surveys the Great Basin region.

1843: Mountain man Jim Bridger founds Fort Bridger in southwestern Wyoming, an important post on the Oregon Trail.

April 1843: Whitman convinces the missionary board to keep the Oregon country missions open.

June 1843: Whitman helps lead one of the first large groups of wagon trains on the Oregon Trail.

October 1843: Whitman arrives back at Waiilatpu. **Marcus** and **Narcissa** provide shelter and supplies for the new pioneers coming into the Oregon country.

June 27, 1844: Joseph Smith is murdered by an anti-Mormon mob.

August 8, 1844: Young becomes the leader of the Mormons.

1844: De Smet founds the St. Francis Xavier Mission on the Willamette River south of Oregon City. It becomes the main supply center for the missions.

January 1845: Illinois revokes the charter of the Mormon city of Nauvoo.

1845: Mexican Californians rebel against rule by Mexico and drive out their colonial governor.

1845: De Smet is removed from his position heading the Rocky Mountain Mission.

Mid-1840s: Miles Goodyear builds a fort at Ogden, Utah.

January 1846: McLoughlin resigns from the Hudson's Bay Company.

May 13, 1846: The United States declares war on Mexico over territory in Texas and the Southwest.

June 15, 1846: The United States and Great Britain agree to set the boundary between the U.S. and Canada at the 49th parallel (the present boundary), ending several years of disputes that threatened war.

July 4, 1846: With the support of Captain John C. Frémont's troops, Americans in California declare the Bear Flag Republic.

April 1847: Young leaves the Mormon camp at Winter Quarters for the Utah region with an advance group.

July 1847: Young's advance group of Mormons reaches the Salt Lake Valley.

November 29, 1847: Marcus and Narcissa Whitman and 11 others are massacred by Cayuses at Waiilatpu.

December 5, 1847: Young is elected president of the Mormon Church.

January 1848: Sutter's sawmill manager, James Marshall, finds gold at his sawmill.

February 2, 1848: The Treaty of Guadalupe Hidalgo gives the United States vast amounts of land in Texas and the Southwest, including parts of New Mexico, Arizona, Wyoming, and Colorado, and all of Utah, Nevada, and California.

August 14, 1848: The Oregon Territory, which includes Oregon, Washington, Idaho, and part of Montana and Wyoming, is created.

September 1848: The first wave of the great migration of Mormons to Salt Lake City is completed.

1849: The California gold rush begins.

1850: The Utah Territory is organized with Young as governor.

1850: The New Mexico Territory is formed.

1850: McLoughlin loses his claim to his land in Oregon City.

September 9, 1850: California becomes the 31st state in the Union. Sacramento is made the capital in 1854.

1851: De Smet draws a map showing tribal boundaries and landholdings after treaty negotiations between the Plains Indians and the U.S. government.

1853: The Washington Territory is established, carved out of the Oregon Territory.

December 30, 1853: The Gadsden Purchase enlarges New Mexico and Arizona.

1857: Young is removed as territorial governor of Utah.

September 3, 1857: McLoughlin dies at the age of 72.

September 11, 1857: In what is known as the Mountain Meadows Massacre, Mormons and Indians in southwestern Utah slaughter a party of pioneers heading to California.

1858: Gold is discovered at Cherry Creek, near what is now Denver, Colorado.

February 14, 1859: Oregon joins the United States as the 33rd state, with its capital at Salem.

1859: Silver and gold are discovered in the Utah Territory.

1859: The Comstock Lode, a silver lode, is discovered in what becomes Nevada.

May-June 1859: De Smet helps negotiate peace between the U.S. government and the Indians of the Northwest.

1861: The Nevada Territory is formed.

1861: The Colorado Territory is organized.

1863: The Arizona Territory is formed.

1863: The Idaho Territory (including Montana) is organized.

1864: The Montana Territory is formed.

October 31, 1864: Nevada becomes the 36th state in the United States, with its capital at Carson City.

1867: Alaska is purchased from Russia by the United States.

1868: De Smet intercedes to help bring peace between Sitting Bull and the Sioux and the U.S. government.

1869: The transcontinental railroad is completed.

May 23, 1873: De Smet dies in St. Louis at the age of 72.

June 25, 1876: The Sioux defeat George Armstrong Custer at the Battle of Little Big Horn in Montana. The Sioux are nevertheless soon put on reservations.

August 1, 1876: Colorado becomes the 38th state, with Denver as its capital.

1877: Chief Joseph and the Nez Perces are defeated and put on reservations.

1877: Silver-bearing ore is discovered near Leadville, Colorado.

August 29, 1877: Young dies in Salt Lake City at the age of 76.

June 1880: Sutter dies at the age of 77.

1883: Railroad lines to the Northwest are completed.

1886: Apache leader Geronimo surrenders to the United States, ending Apache resistance to white settlement in Arizona.

1887: The United States establishes a naval base in Hawaii at Pearl Harbor.

November 8, 1889: Montana enters the Union as the 41st state, with its capital at Helena.

November 11, 1889: Washington is the 42nd state admitted to the United States, with Olympia as its capital.

1890: The Mormon Church renounces plural marriage.

July 3, 1890: Idaho becomes the 43rd state in the Union, with its capital at Boise.

January 1893: The Hawaiian monarchy is overthrown and Hawaii becomes a U.S. protectorate governed by Americans.

January 4, 1896: Utah becomes the 45th state in the Union, with Salt Lake City as the capital.

July 1898: The United States annexes Hawaii.

1900: The Hawaii Territory is formed, governed by Sanford Dole.

January 6, 1912: New Mexico becomes the 47th state, with its capital at Santa Fe.

February 14, 1912: Arizona joins the Union as the 48th state, with Phoenix as its capital.

1912: The Alaska Territory is established.

1934: Serra is nominated for canonization in the Roman Catholic Church.

January 3, 1959: Alaska becomes the 49th state, with its capital at Juneau.

August 21, 1959: Hawaii joins the Union as the 50th state. Its capital is Honolulu.

September 25, 1988: Serra is beatified, the last step before sainthood.

Source Notes

Quoted passages are noted by page and order of citation. Spelling and some capitalizations are modernized.

Chapter One
p. 13: Dumas Malone, ed., *Dictionary of American Biography* (New York: Scribner's, 1939).
p. 15: Malone, *Dictionary of American Biography*.
p. 16: Robert McGeath, *Colony in the Wilderness* (Santa Fe: Sunstone Press, 1990), 28.
p. 17: McGeath, *Colony in the Wilderness*, 29-30.
p. 20 (margin): McGeath, *Colony in the Wilderness*, 33.
p. 26 (caption): David J. Weber, *The Spanish Frontier in North America* (New Haven, Conn.: Yale University Press, 1992), 82.

Chapter Two
p. 34 (first): Herbert Eugene Bolton, *Rim of Christendom: A Biography of Eusebio Francisco Kino, Pacific Coast Pioneer* (New York: Russell & Russell, 1960), 38.
p. 34 (second): Bolton, *Rim of Christendom*, 70.
p. 35 (caption): Bolton, *Rim of Christendom*, 71.
p. 37 (first margin): Herbert Eugene Bolton, *The Padre on Horseback: A Sketch of Eusebio Francisco Kino, S. J., Apostle to the Pimas* (San Francisco: The Sonora Press, 1932), 82.
p. 37 (second margin): Bolton, *The Padre on Horseback*, 82-83.
p. 39 (both): Bolton, *The Padre on Horseback*, 52.
p. 41 (caption): Ernest J. Burrus, S. J., *Kino and Manje, Explorers of Sonora and Arizona: Their Vision of the Future*, vol. X of *Sources and Studies for the History of the Americas* (St. Louis: Jesuit Historical Institute, 1971), 95.
p. 42 (first margin): Bolton, *The Padre on Horseback*, 84.
p. 42 (second margin): Bolton, *The Padre on Horseback*, 83.
p. 43: Bolton, *Rim of Christendom*, 70.
p. 44 (margin): Bolton, *The Padre on Horseback*, 84.

Chapter Three
p. 47 (caption): George Wharton James, ed., *Francisco Palóu's Life and Apostolic Labors of the Venerable Father Junípero Serra* (Pasadena, Calif.: George Wharton James, 1913), xxiii.
p. 49 (first margin): James, ed., *Palóu's Life of Serra*, 4.
p. 49 (second margin): James, ed., *Palóu's Life of Serra*, 5.
p. 49 (third margin): Marion A. Habig, O. F. M., and Francis Borgia Steck, O. F. M., *Man of Greatness: Father Junípero Serra* (Chicago: Franciscan Herald Press, 1964), 21.
p. 53 (first margin): Sean Dolan, *Junípero Serra* (New York: Chelsea House, 1991), 94.
p. 53 (second margin): M. V. Woodgate, *Junípero Serra: Apostle of California, 1713-1784* (Westminster, Md.: The Newman Press, 1966), 65-66.

p. 55 (first margin): Herbert Eugene Bolton, *Fray Juan Crespí: Missionary Explorer on the Pacific Coast, 1769-1794* (New York: AMS Press, 1971), 17.

p. 55 (second margin): Dolan, *Junípero Serra*, 100.

p. 58: Habig and Steck, *Man of Greatness*, 161.

Chapter Four

p. 62 (margin): J. Peter Zollinger, *Sutter: The Man and His Empire* (Gloucester, Mass.: Peter Smith, 1967), 10.

p. 63 (margin): Zollinger, *Sutter*, 18.

p. 64 (margin): Zollinger, *Sutter*, 36-37.

p. 64 (caption): Zollinger, *Sutter*, 54.

p. 65 (margin): John Bakeless, *America as Seen by Its First Explorers* (New York: Dover Publications, 1961), 392.

p. 65: Zollinger, *Sutter*, 57.

p. 66: Richard Dillon, *Fool's Gold: The Decline and Fall of Captain John Sutter of California* (New York: Coward-McCann, 1967), 89.

p. 67 (margin): Zollinger, *Sutter*, 80.

p. 68 (caption): Zollinger, *Sutter*, 117.

p. 69: Zollinger, *Sutter*, 112.

p. 72: Ted Morgan, *A Shovel of Stars* (New York: Simon & Schuster, 1995), 166.

p. 73 (margin): Zollinger, *Sutter*, 265.

p. 76 (margin): John A. Sutter, "The Discovery of Gold in California," *Hutchings' California Magazine* (November 1857).

Chapter Five

p. 82 (margin): Dorothy Nafus Morrison, *The Eagle and the Fort: The Story of John McLoughlin* (New York: Atheneum, 1979), 15.

p. 87 (caption): Robert G. Cleland, *This Reckless Breed of Men: The Trappers and Fur Traders of the Southwest* (New York: Knopf, 1950), 312-313.

p. 87 (margin): LeRoy R. Hafen, ed., *Mountain Men and Fur Traders of the Far West* (Lincoln: University of Nebraska Press, 1982), 115-116.

p. 88 (both): Morrison, *The Eagle and the Fort*, 61.

p. 91: Morrison, *The Eagle and the Fort*, 115.

p. 93 (first margin): Hafen, *Mountain Men and Fur Traders*, 119.

p. 93 (second margin): Morrison, *The Eagle and the Fort*, 144.

p. 94: Morrison, *The Eagle and the Fort*, 146.

Chapter Six

p. 99: Clifford M. Drury, *Marcus and Narcissa Whitman and the Opening of Old Oregon*, vol. I (Glendale, Calif.: The Arthur H. Clark Company, 1973), 161.

p. 103 (margin): Drury, *Marcus and Narcissa Whitman*, vol. I, 112.

p. 103 (first): Drury, *Marcus and Narcissa Whitman*, vol. I, 109.

p. 103 (second): Drury, *Marcus and Narcissa Whitman*, vol. I, 110.

p. 104 (margin): Drury, *Marcus and Narcissa Whitman*, vol. I, 132.

p. 105: Morgan, *A Shovel of Stars*, 139.

p. 107 (caption): Drury, *Marcus and Narcissa Whitman*, vol. I, 187.

p. 108 (margin): Drury, *Marcus and Narcissa Whitman*, vol. I, 200.

p. 109 (caption): Drury, *Marcus and Narcissa Whitman*, vol. I, 213.

p. 110 (first margin): Drury, *Marcus and Narcissa Whitman*, vol. I, 233.

p. 110 (second margin): Drury, *Marcus and Narcissa Whitman*, vol. I, 353.

p. 110 (first and second): Drury, *Marcus and Narcissa Whitman*, vol. I, 225-226.

p. 110 (third): Drury, *Marcus and Narcissa Whitman*, vol. I, 241.

p. 113 (caption): Drury, *Marcus and Narcissa Whitman*, vol. II, 42.

p. 114 (caption): Drury, *Marcus and Narcissa Whitman*, vol. II, 53.

p. 118 (margin): Drury, *Marcus and Narcissa Whitman*, vol. II, 196.

Chapter Seven

p. 121: Robert C. Carriker, *Father Peter John De Smet: Jesuit in the West* (Norman: University of Oklahoma Press, 1995), 3.

p. 122 (margin): Carriker, *Father Peter John De Smet*, 4.

p. 123 (margin): Carriker, *Father Peter John De Smet*, 11.

p. 125 (margin): Carriker, *Father Peter John De Smet*, 24.

p. 125 (both): Carriker, *Father Peter John De Smet*, 22-23.

p. 127 (margin): John Killoren, S. J., *"Come, Blackrobe": De Smet and the Indian Tragedy* (Norman: University of Oklahoma Press, 1994), 62.

p. 127 (both): Killoren, *"Come, Blackrobe,"* 61-62.

p. 130 (caption): John Upton Terrell, *Black Robe: The Life of Pierre-Jean De Smet, Missionary, Explorer & Pioneer* (Garden City, N.Y.: Doubleday, 1964), 148.

p. 130: Carriker, *Father Peter John De Smet*, 48.

p. 136 (margin): Carriker, *Father Peter John De Smet*, 208.

p. 137 (caption): Carriker, *Father Peter John De Smet*, 223.

Chapter Eight

p. 139: Stanley P. Hirshson, *The Lion of the Lord: A Biography of Brigham Young* (New York: Knopf, 1969), 85.

p. 140 (margin): Hirshson, *The Lion of the Lord*, 6.

p. 141 (margin): Hirshson, *The Lion of the Lord*, 7.

p. 142 (margin): Irving Stone, *Men to Match My Mountains: The Opening of the Far West, 1840-1900* (Garden City, N.Y.: Doubleday, 1956), 95.

p. 144 (margin): Stone, *Men to Match My Mountains*, 157.

p. 144: Leonard J. Arrington, *Brigham Young: American Moses* (New York: Knopf, 1985), 100.

p. 145: Arrington, *Brigham Young*, 114.

p. 149: Hirshson, *The Lion of the Lord*, 85.

p. 150 (caption): Stone, *Men to Match My Mountains*, 95.

p. 151 (caption): Stone, *Men to Match My Mountains*, 178.

p. 152 (margin): Hirshson, *The Lion of the Lord*, 153.

p. 152: Hirshson, *The Lion of the Lord*, 152.

p. 153 (margin): Arrington, *Brigham Young*, 258.

p. 155: Hirshson, *The Lion of the Lord*, 320.

Bibliography

Ainsworth, Edward M., and Katherine Ainsworth. *In the Shade of the Juniper Tree*. Garden City, N.Y.: Doubleday, 1970.

Arrington, Leonard J. *Brigham Young: American Moses*. New York: Knopf, 1985.

Bakeless, John. *America as Seen by Its First Explorers*. New York: Dover Publications, 1961.

Billington, Ray Allen. *Westward Expansion*. New York: Macmillan, 1982.

Bolton, Herbert Eugene. *Fray Juan Crespí: Missionary Explorer on the Pacific Coast, 1769-1794*. New York: AMS Press, 1971.

—————. *The Padre on Horseback: A Sketch of Eusebio Francisco Kino, S. J., Apostle to the Pimas*. San Francisco: The Sonora Press, 1932.

—————. *Rim of Christendom: A Biography of Eusebio Francisco Kino, Pacific Coast Pioneer*. New York: Russell & Russell, 1960.

Bringhurst, Newell G. *Brigham Young and the Expanding American Frontier*. Boston: Little, Brown, 1986.

Burrus, Ernest J., S. J. *Kino and Manje, Explorers of Sonora and Arizona: Their Vision of the Future*. Vol. X of *Sources and Studies for the History of the Americas*. St. Louis: Jesuit Historical Institute, 1971.

Carriker, Robert C. *Father Peter John De Smet: Jesuit in the West*. Norman: University of Oklahoma Press, 1995.

Cleland, Robert G. *This Reckless Breed of Men: The Trappers and Fur Traders of the Southwest*. New York: Knopf, 1950.

Corle, Edwin. *The Gila: River of the Southwest*. New York: Rinehart, 1951.

Dana, Julian. *Sutter of California*. New York: Halcyon House, 1938.

De Nevi, Don, and Noel Francis Moholy. *Junípero Serra: The Illustrated Story of the Franciscan Founder of California's Missions*. New York: Harper & Row, 1985.

Dillon, Richard. *Fool's Gold: The Decline and Fall of Captain John Sutter of California*. New York: Coward-McCann, 1967.

Dolan, Sean. *Junípero Serra*. New York: Chelsea House, 1991.

Drury, Clifford M. *Marcus and Narcissa Whitman and the Opening of Old Oregon*. Vols. I-II. Glendale, Calif.: The Arthur H. Clark Company, 1973.

Gudde, Erwin G. *Sutter's Own Story: The Life of General John Augustus Sutter and the History of New Helvetia in the Sacramento Valley*. New York: G. P. Putnam's Sons, 1936.

Habig, Marion A., O. F. M., and Francis Borgia Steck, O. F. M. *Man of Greatness: Father Junípero Serra*. Chicago: Franciscan Herald Press, 1964.

Hafen, LeRoy R. *Mountain Men and Fur Traders of the Far West*. Lincoln: University of Nebraska Press, 1982.

Hawgood, John A. *America's Western Frontiers*. New York: Knopf, 1967.

Hirshson, Stanley P. *The Lion of the Lord: A Biography of Brigham Young*. New York: Knopf, 1969.

Holman, Frederick V. *Dr. John McLoughlin: The Father of Oregon*. Cleveland: The Arthur H. Clark Company, 1907.

James, George Wharton, Ed. *Francisco Palóu's Life and Apostolic Labors of the Venerable Father Junípero Serra*. Pasadena, Calif.: George Wharton James, 1913.

Johnson, Robert C. *John McLoughlin: Patriarch of the Northwest*. Portland, Ore.: Metropolitan Press, 1935.

Jones, Nard. *The Great Command: The Story of Marcus and Narcissa Whitman and the Oregon Country Pioneers*. Boston: Little, Brown, 1959.

Killoren, John, S. J. *"Come Blackrobe": De Smet and the Indian Tragedy*. Norman: University of Oklahoma Press, 1994.

McGeath, Robert. *Colony in the Wilderness*. Santa Fe: Sunstone Press, 1990.

Merk, Frederick. *History of the Westward Movement*. New York: Knopf, 1978.

Montgomery, Richard G. *The White-Headed Eagle: John McLoughlin, Builder of an Empire*. New York: Macmillan, 1934.

Morgan, Dale L. *The Great Salt Lake*. Indianapolis: Bobbs-Merrill, 1947.

Morgan, Ted. *A Shovel of Stars*. New York: Simon & Schuster, 1995.

Morrison, Dorothy Nafus. *The Eagle and the Fort: The Story of John McLoughlin*. New York: Atheneum, 1979.

Simmons, Marc. *The Last Conquistador: Juan de Oñate and the Settling of the Far Southwest*. Norman: University of Oklahoma Press, 1991.

Stone, Irving. *Men to Match My Mountains: The Opening of the Far West, 1840-1900*. Garden City, N.Y.: Doubleday, 1956.

Sutter, John A. "The Discovery of Gold in California." *Hutchings' California Magazine* (November 1857).

Sutter, John A., Jr. *Statement Regarding Early California Experiences*. Ed. Allan R. Ottley. Sacramento: Sacramento Book Collectors Club, 1943.

Terrell, John Upton. *Black Robe: The Life of Pierre-Jean De Smet, Missionary, Explorer & Pioneer*. Garden City, N.Y.: Doubleday, 1964.

Trimble, Marshall. *Arizona: A Cavalcade of History*. Garden City, N.Y.: Doubleday, 1977.

Weber, David J. *The Spanish Frontier in North America*. New Haven, Conn.: Yale University Press, 1992.

Webster, Kimball. *The Gold Seekers of '49: A Personal Narrative of the Overland Trail and Adventures in California and Oregon from 1849 to 1854*. Manchester, N.H.: Standard Book Company, 1917.

Wellman, Paul I. *Glory, God and Gold: A Narrative History*. Garden City: N.Y.: Doubleday, 1954.

Woodgate, M. V. *Junípero Serra: Apostle of California, 1713-1784*. Westminster, Md.: The Newman Press, 1966.

Zollinger, J. Peter. *Sutter: The Man and His Empire*. Gloucester, Mass.: Peter Smith, 1967.

Index

De Smet, Josse-Arnaud (father), 122

De Smet, Marie-Jeanne (mother), 122

De Smet, Peter (Pierre-Jean), 115; conversion of Indians by, 127, 130, 131, 132, 134, 137; death of, 137; early years of, 121-122; as fundraiser, 124, 125, 128, 131, 137; health of, 124, 126, 136; as Jesuit priest, 11, 123-125, 131, 132; missions established by, 11, 130, 131-132; in Missouri, 123, 125, 128, 134; as peacemaker, 134, 136, 137; relationship of, with Indians, 11, 123, 125, 127, 128, 130, 131, 133, 134, 136, 137; work of, among Flathead Indians, 126, 127, 128, 130

De Smet, Rosalie (sister), 123

Dole, Sanford, 79

Dolores, Mission, 39, 41, 42, 44

Dominguez, Francisco Atanasio, 148

Drake, Francis, 54

Eells, Cushing, 112

1812, War of, 84, 108

Escalante, Silvestre Vélez de, 148

"Fifty-Four Forty or Fight," 93

Flathead Indians, 7, 127, 128, 129, 130, 134, 136; request of, for missionaries, 106, 108, 126

Florida, 9, 48

Fort Laramie Treaty, 136

'Forty-Niners, 74

Franciscan order, 47, 48, 49, 51, 52; missionaries of, 10, 16, 18, 23, 25, 49, 50, 53, 148; missions established by, 10, 53, 55-57. See also Serra, Junípero

Frémont, John C., 70, 71, 148

fur trade, 10, 44, 64, 67, 70, 81, 82, 105, 148, 157; British involvement in, 78, 81, 82, 84, 85, 86, 87, 88, 89, 108; decline of, 105, 128; Hudson's Bay Company and, 81, 83, 85, 88, 93, 108, 110, 117, 129; Indians in, 104, 127; mountain men and, 104-105; North West Company and, 82, 83, 84, 108, 129; Pacific Fur Company and, 83, 84, 86, 108; rendezvous in, 104, 105, 106, 128; Russian involvement in, 54, 55, 69, 77-78; U.S. involvement in, 83, 84, 85, 86, 88, 89, 103, 108

Gadsden Purchase, 29, 45

Gálvez, José de, 53, 55

Garcés, F. T. H., 44

George, Fort, 81, 83, 84, 85, 86

Gerstl, Adam, 34

gold, 19, 34, 35, 38, 78, 119, 156, 157; discovery of, in California, 71-72; rush, 61, 73, 74, 75, 76, 97, 115, 135, 156

Goodyear, Miles, 148

Gray, Robert, 84, 90, 108

Gray, William H., 106

Great Awakening, Second, 100

Great Britain, 56; conflict of, with U.S. in Northwest, 84, 85, 86, 88-89, 90, 93, 94, 97, 108; involvement of, in fur trade, 10, 78, 81, 82, 83, 84, 85, 86, 87, 88, 89, 108; New Albion claimed by, 2, 54

Great Salt Lake, 146; valley of, 146, 147, 149, 150

Green River Rendezvous, 104, 105, 106, 107, 108, 127

Guadalupe Hidalgo, Treaty of, 29, 45, 150

Guaymas Indians, 37

Hall, Fort, 115, 128, 129

handcart migrants, 151-152

Hawaiian Islands, 61, 64, 77, 78-79

Hawikuh pueblo, 19

Hohokam Indians, 7, 38

Hopi Indians, 20, 38

Hudson Bay, 81

Hudson's Bay Company, 11, 93, 108, 110, 117, 118, 129, 130-131; McLoughlin employed by, 81, 83, 85-89, 91-94

Hupa Indians, 54

Idaho, 105, 115, 151, 156; De Smet in, 11, 127, 128, 132, 133; gold rush in, 135; Indians in, 7, 129, 135; missions in, 11, 132, 133; as state, 135; as U.S. territory, 97, 135

Inca Indians, 9

Indians, American, 10, 11, 91, 114, 122, 153; alcoholism among, 125-126, 128; ancient cultures of, 7, 18, 38, 39, 54, 84, 108, 129, 148; devastated by European diseases, 59, 108, 117; effect on, of missions, 59; in fur trade, 104, 127; in Mexico, 9, 14, 15, 16; missionaries sought by, 101, 103, 106, 108, 126; in Northwest, 84, 131. See also individual tribes

Iroquois Indians, 126, 127

Jefferson, Thomas, 90

Jesuit order, 10, 32, 33, 34, 42; banned from Spanish colonies, 44, 53; missionaries of, 10, 32, 33-34, 121, 123, 124, 128; missions established by, 11, 37, 39, 40-42, 128, 130, 131-132, 134. See also De Smet, Peter; Kino, Eusebio; Society of Jesus

John Paul II (Roman Catholic pope), 59

Joseph (Nez Perce chief), 135

Judd, G. P., 78

Kalispel Indians, 129, 131, 132, 134

Kamehameha I (king of Hawaiian Islands), 78

About the Author

Kieran Doherty is an experienced journalist and business writer as well as a nonfiction writer for young adults. He is the author of four other **Shaping America** books, *Puritans, Pilgrims, and Merchants: Founders of the Northeastern Colonies*; *Soldiers, Cavaliers, and Planters: Settlers of the Southeastern Colonies*; *Ranchers, Homesteaders, and Traders: Frontiersmen of the South-Central States*; and *Voyageurs, Lumberjacks, and Farmers: Pioneers of the Midwest*. An avid sailor, he lives in Boynton Beach, Florida, with his wife, Lynne.

Photo Credits